Voyager

Set In Soul

© 2020 Tatiana Media LLC in partnership with Set In Soul LLC

ISBN #: 978-1-949874-94-5

Published by Tatiana Media LLC

For general information on our other products and services, please contact our Customer Support within the United States at support@setinsoul.com.

Tatiana Media LLC as well as Set In Soul LLC publishes its books in a variety of electronic formats. Some content that appears in print may not be available in electronic books.

This Journal Belongs To

_____

Dedicated To The
Wanderer Within Me
Who Keeps Growing
And Loving.

Table Of Contents

How To Use This Journal

It's time to plan and go on your next adventure. Many of us want to see the wonders of this amazing world. We choose to travel to visit new places, taste exotic flavors, see interesting architecture, experience a culture different from ours as well as meet new people and make new friends. It's through traveling you create memories with friends, family, and/or coworkers. The memories you create are kept alive with tickets, pictures, souvenirs, maps and other forms of memorabilia. It is also through traveling that you do not just discover the world but you also discover yourself. In the discovery of you …. new thoughts are created, refreshing realizations are formed and unique moments of inspiration happen all because of the places and events you have decided to travel to. It is important to write down or sketch out these thoughts as well as take and keep physical pictures that reflect your moments and your memories. This travel journal serves as the perfect place to do just that.

Because traveling has no limits, your creativity also has no limits. You can use this journal to choose and plan your next travel adventure. From the start of your trip to the end of your trip you can write down your journey to your destination, capture your actual adventure and retell your story of your trip back home. This journal is meant for you to travel with so you can capture big and small moments that you can look back at later and share with your loved ones. It is also recommended that you take pictures and attach them to each trip story. This is also your opportunity to sketch out anything that the camera couldn't capture as well as write down the names and numbers of your new friends and record dates of important events you've attended. Whatever deserves to be preserved into memory, let your journal also be the space for it.

We recommend using this journal as soon as you have decided where you are going. From there you can plan the details of your local, national or international trip then carry this journal along your adventure to write down your thoughts and anything you would like to be reminded of. The maps of the different countries are there for you to plan your next trip and color in places you have already visited. Whether this is your first time traveling or you are an experienced traveler, this is your time to discover the voyager within you.

The Continents

Arctic Ocean

Alaska

Yukon

Northwest Territories

Gulf of Alaska

Canada

British Columbia

Alberta

Saskatch

Washington

Montana

Oregon

Idaho

Wyoming

Nevada

Utah

Colora

California

Arizona

New Mexi

Pacific Ocean

Hawaii

North America

Baffin Bay

Greenland

Davis Strait

Iceland

Hudson Bay

Québec

Newfoundland and Labrador

Ontario

nesota

Wisconsin

New Brunswick
Prince Edward Island
Maine
Nova Scotia

Saint Pierre and Miquelon

Michigan

Iowa

Illinois

Indiana

Ohio

Vermont
New Hampshire
New York
Massachusetts
Connecticut
Pennsylvania
New Jersey
Maryland
West Virginia
Delaware

Missouri

Kentucky

Virginia

Atlantic Ocean

Tennessee

North Carolina

Arkansas

South Carolina

Mississippi

Alabama

Georgia

Bermuda

Louisiana

Florida

Gulf of Mexico

Bahamas

Cuba Turks and Caicos Islands

Cayman Islands

Jamaica

Haiti Dominican Republic

Puerto Rico Netherlands Antilles

Belize

Guatemala

Caribbean Sea

Guadeloupe

Honduras

Martinique

El Salvador

Nicaragua

Saint Lucia

Aruba

Grenada

Costa Rica

Trinidad and Tobago

Panama

N
W E
S

9

South America

Atlantic Ocean

North America

Venezuela

Guyana

Suriname

French Guiana

Colombia

Ecuador

Brazil

Peru

South America

Bolivia

Pacific Ocean

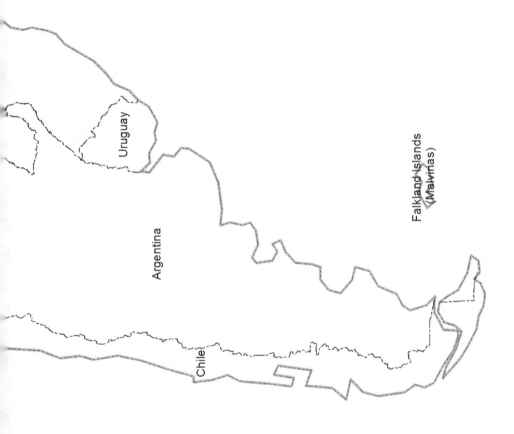

South Georgia
South Sandwich Islands

Uruguay

Argentina

Falkland Islands
(Malvinas)

Chile

GreenLand

Iceland

Faroe Islands

Norway

North Sea

Denmark

Ireland

United Kingdom

Netherlands

Germany

Belgium

Luxembourg

Jersey

Atlantic Ocean

France

Liechtenstein
Switzerland

San Marino
Italy

Monaco

Vatican C.

Andorra

Portugal

Spain

Mediterranean Sea

Gibraltar

AFRICA

Europe

Arctic Ocean

Finland

Estonia

Latvia

Lithuania

Belarus

Russia

Ukraine

Republic of Moldova

Romania

Bulgaria

Turkey

Black Sea

Caspian Sea

ASIA

ASIA

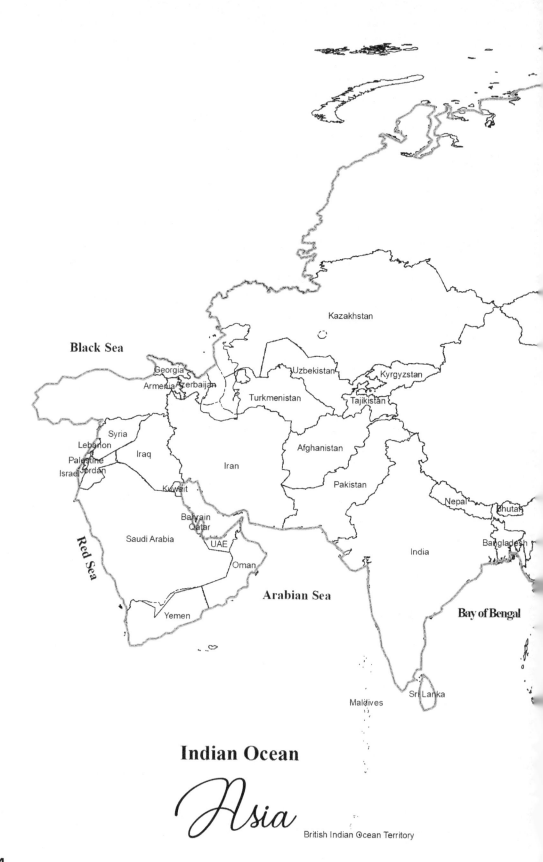

Black Sea

Kazakhstan

Georgia

Armenia Azerbaijan

Uzbekistan

Kyrgyzstan

Turkmenistan

Tajikistan

Syria

Lebanon

Iraq

Afghanistan

Palestine

Iran

Israel Jordan

Pakistan

Kuwait

Bahrain

Nepal

Qatar

Bhutan

Saudi Arabia

UAE

Bangladesh

Red Sea

Oman

India

Arabian Sea

Yemen

Bay of Bengal

Sri Lanka

Maldives

Indian Ocean

Asia

British Indian Ocean Territory

14

Arctic Ocean

Russia

Bering Sea

Sea of Okhotsk

lia

North Korea

Sea of Japan

South Korea

Japan

Pacific Ocean

East China Sea

Taiwan

Hong Kong

Philippines

nbodia

Viet Nam

South China Sea

Brunei Darussalam

Malaysia

ore

Indonesia

Timor-Leste

N
15

Africa

Arabian Sea

Somalia

Djibouti

Eritrea

Ethiopia

Red Sea

Egypt

Sudan

Mediterranean Sea

Libyan Arab Jamahiriya

Chad

Central African Republic

Tunisia

Niger

Nigeria

Cameroon

Algeria

Mali

Burkina Faso

Benin

Togo

Ghana

Cote d'Ivoire

Morocco

Mauritania

Guinea

Sierra Leone

Liberia

Western Sahara

Senegal

Gambia

Guinea-Bissau

Gulf of Guinea

Cape Verde

16

Atlantic Ocean

Saint Helena

Mauritius
Reunion

Madagascar

Comoros
Mayotte

Mozambique Channel

Mozambique

Malawi

Zimbabwe

Swaziland

Lesotho

Zambia

Botswana

South Africa

Angola

Namibia

Northern Mariana Islands

Guam

Palau

Micronesia

Papua New Guinea

Arafura Sea

Ashmore and Cartier Islands

Coral Sea

Timor Sea

Northern Territory

Coral Sea Islands

Queensland

Australia

Western Australia

South Australia

New South Wales

Jervis Bay Territory

ACT

Victoria

Indian Ocean

Oceania

Tasmania

Minor Outlying Islands

of Marshall Islands

Kiribati

Nauru

Tuvalu   Tokelau

Samoa
Wallis and Futuna Islands American Samoa

Vanuatu

French Polynesia

Fiji
Niue

ledonia
Tonga   Cook Islands

Pacific Ocean

rfolk Island

New Zealand

N
W   E
S

Pacific Ocean

Atlantic Ocean

B

NORTH

Antarctica

French Southern and Antarctic Lands

Indian Ocean

Heard Island and McDonald Islands

ca

Places I Have Traveled To

Places I Have Traveled To

A Continuation Of The Places I Have Traveled To

People I
Have Met

People I Have Met (Write Their Names And Contact Information)

Upcoming Travel Plans

Upcoming Travel Plans

A Continuation Of My Upcoming Travel Plans

A Continuation Of My Upcoming Travel Plans

A Continuation Of My Upcoming Travel Plans

A Continuation Of My Upcoming Travel Plans

A Continuation Of My Upcoming Travel Plans

My Personal Traveling Experiences

My Personal Traveling Experiences

I Travel (How Often):

I Love To Travel Because (Answer If Applicable):

I Want To Start Traveling Because (Answer If Applicable):

I Speak (How Many Languages):

I Can Write (Write Down How Many Languages I Can Write In And List Them):

My Personal Traveling Experiences

I Have Traveled On My Own To These Places:

I Have Traveled For My Job To These Places:

I Have Traveled With The Military To These Places:

I Have Traveled With My Family To These Places:

I Have Traveled With My Church To These Places:

My Personal Traveling Experiences

I Have Traveled With My Friends To These Places:

I Have Traveled With My Romantic Partner(s) To These Places:

Traveling Makes Me Feel:

Through Traveling, I Have Learned:

Because Of Traveling, I Am Not Scared To:

My Personal Traveling Experiences

I Am Much More Open To:

Things I Tell Other People Who Want To Travel:

When I Travel I Always Bring:

I Started Traveling At The Age Of:

Favorite Place I Have Traveled To So Far:

My Personal Traveling Experiences

Least Favorite Place I Have Traveled To So Far:

I Like To Stay At:

Places I Would Like To Visit/See When I Am Traveling:

When Traveling, I Like To:

New Languages I Have Learned From My Travels:

My Personal Traveling Experiences

The Most Valuable Thing I Have Bought While Traveling:

The Most Valuable Thing That Was Given To Me While Traveling:

I Like To Support:

I Always Look Forward To:

I Always Hope:

My Personal Traveling Experiences

The Person I Always Want To Travel With (Answer If Applicable):

I Am Able To Afford My Trips By:

I Always Wish I Could Bring Home:

I Normally Travel For (Write How Many Days):

One Of My Most Memorable Trips:

My Personal Traveling Experiences

When I Am Away From Home, I Miss:

When I First Started Traveling, I Was Told:

A Typical Day Of Traveling With Me:

A Few Of My Favorite Resturants That I Have Discovered When
I Have Traveled:

A Major Event That Happened While I Was Traveling:

My Personal Traveling Experiences

Adventure To Me Means:

What Is More Exciting For Me? The Journey Or The Destination?

Based On My Previous Response, Why?

The Most Adventurous Thing I Have Done So Far:

Places I Want To Go Back To:

My Personal Traveling Experiences

An Unexpected Experience I Had When Traveling:

What I Have Gained Through Traveling:

How Long Does It Take For Me To Plan A Trip?

The Best Part About Planning A Trip:

Something I Did Not Get A Chance To Do Somewhere I Visited
But Wish I Did:

My Personal Traveling Experiences

Road Trips I Have Taken:

How Long Have These Road Trips Lasted?

I Like To Share My Travels With:

I Like To Observe:

I Feel Safe Knowing:

My Personal Traveling Experiences

When I Travel, I Always Remind Myself:

When I Travel, I Usually Forget:

When I Travel, I Often Expect:

Books I Have Read While Traveling (Answer If Applicable):

A Book I Have Read That Has Inspired Me To Travel (Answer If Applicable):

My Personal Traveling Experiences

Songs I Often Listen To When I Travel (Answer If Applicable):

Movies I Often Watch When I Travel (Answer If Applicable):

Travel Hacks

A List Of My Travel Hacks

My Travel Goals

My Travel Goals

A Continuation Of My Travel Goals

Off To My
Next Adventure

Off To My Next Adventure

Date: My Level Of Excitement: 😍 😁 😖 😰

I Am Naming This Trip:

Where Am I Going?

Who Am I Going With?

How Long Is This Trip?

I Plan To Travel By:

Any Layovers Or Detours On This Trip?

If Yes To The Previous Prompt, Where And Why?

Why Does This Trip Matter To Me?

Where Will I Be Staying?

The Reason For This Trip:

My Trip Budget:

I Want To See:

A Top Priority For Me On This Trip:

I Want To Experience:

Will I Have An Itinerary For This Trip Or Will I Just Freestyle My Visit?

I Plan To Learn:

Trip Name:

Location: Arrival Date: Arrival Time: End Of Trip Date:

During This Trip, I Felt: Best Memory Of The Trip:

Foods And Drinks I Enjoyed: I Am Now Inspired To:

Places I Have Visited: What I Would Recommend/Not
                                          Recommend About This Trip:

What I Enjoyed During My Trip: Would I Come Here Again?

What I Did Not Enjoy During My Trip: I Realized:

I Met:

Attach Picture

My Trip Story:

There Is Something Special Waiting For Me.

The Food.
The Cultures.
The Amazing
People.

Off To My Next Adventure

Date: _____ My Level Of Excitement: 😊 😄 😵‍💫 😱

I Am Naming This Trip:

Where Will I Be Staying?

Where Am I Going?

The Reason For This Trip:

Who Am I Going With?

My Trip Budget:

How Long Is This Trip?

I Want To See:

I Plan To Travel By:

A Top Priority For Me On This Trip:

Any Layovers Or Detours On This Trip?

I Want To Experience:

If Yes To The Previous Prompt, Where And Why?

Will I Have An Itinerary For This Trip Or Will I Just Freestyle My Visit?

Why Does This Trip Matter To Me?

I Plan To Learn:

Trip Name:

Location: Arrival Date: Arrival Time: End Of Trip Date:

During This Trip, I Felt:

Best Memory Of The Trip:

Foods And Drinks I Enjoyed:

I Am Now Inspired To:

Places I Have Visited:

What I Would Recommend/Not Recommend About This Trip:

Attach Picture

What I Enjoyed During My Trip:

Would I Come Here Again?

What I Did Not Enjoy During My Trip:

I Realized:

I Met:

My Trip Story:

Off To My Next Adventure

Date: _____ My Level Of Excitement: 😍 😄 😌 😲

I Am Naming This Trip:

Where Will I Be Staying?

Where Am I Going?

The Reason For This Trip:

Who Am I Going With?

My Trip Budget:

How Long Is This Trip?

I Want To See:

I Plan To Travel By:

A Top Priority For Me On This Trip:

Any Layovers Or Detours On This Trip?

I Want To Experience:

If Yes To The Previous Prompt, Where And Why?

Will I Have An Itinerary For This Trip Or Will I Just Freestyle My Visit?

Why Does This Trip Matter To Me?

I Plan To Learn:

Trip Name:

Location: Arrival Date: Arrival Time: End Of Trip Date:

During This Trip, I Felt: Best Memory Of The Trip:

Foods And Drinks I Enjoyed: I Am Now Inspired To:

Places I Have Visited: What I Would Recommend/Not
                                              Recommend About This Trip:

What I Enjoyed During My Trip: Would I Come Here Again?

What I Did Not Enjoy During My Trip: I Realized:

I Met:

Attach Picture

My Trip Story:

Right Before A Trip I Like To....

My Spirit Has Traveled To These Places Way Before I Physically Got There.

Off To My Next Adventure

Date: My Level Of Excitement: 😍 😁 😔 😰

I Am Naming This Trip:

Where Am I Going?

Who Am I Going With?

How Long Is This Trip?

I Plan To Travel By:

Any Layovers Or Detours On This Trip?

If Yes To The Previous Prompt, Where And Why?

Why Does This Trip Matter To Me?

Where Will I Be Staying?

The Reason For This Trip:

My Trip Budget:

I Want To See:

A Top Priority For Me On This Trip:

I Want To Experience:

Will I Have An Itinerary For This Trip Or Will I Just Freestyle My Visit?

I Plan To Learn:

Trip Name:

Location: Arrival Date: Arrival Time: End Of Trip Date:

During This Trip, I Felt:

Best Memory Of The Trip:

Foods And Drinks I Enjoyed:

I Am Now Inspired To:

Places I Have Visited:

What I Would Recommend/Not Recommend About This Trip:

What I Enjoyed During My Trip:

Would I Come Here Again?

What I Did Not Enjoy During My Trip:

I Realized:

I Met:

Attach Picture

My Trip Story:

I Like To Pack....

My Packing Must-Haves....

My Travel Notes

Off To My Next Adventure

Date: My Level Of Excitement:

I Am Naming This Trip:

Where Will I Be Staying?

Where Am I Going?

The Reason For This Trip:

Who Am I Going With?

My Trip Budget:

How Long Is This Trip?

I Want To See:

I Plan To Travel By:

A Top Priority For Me On This Trip:

Any Layovers Or Detours On This Trip?

I Want To Experience:

If Yes To The Previous Prompt, Where And Why?

Will I Have An Itinerary For This Trip Or Will I Just Freestyle My Visit?

Why Does This Trip Matter To Me?

I Plan To Learn:

Trip Name:

Location: Arrival Date: Arrival Time: End Of Trip Date:

During This Trip, I Felt: Best Memory Of The Trip:

Foods And Drinks I Enjoyed: I Am Now Inspired To:

Places I Have Visited: What I Would Recommend/Not
                                           Recommend About This Trip:

What I Enjoyed During My Trip: Would I Come Here Again?

What I Did Not Enjoy During My Trip: I Realized:

I Met:

Attach Picture

My Trip Story:

Off To My Next Adventure

Date: _____   My Level Of Excitement: 😍 😁 😌 😨

I Am Naming This Trip:

Where Will I Be Staying?

Where Am I Going?

The Reason For This Trip:

Who Am I Going With?

My Trip Budget:

How Long Is This Trip?

I Want To See:

I Plan To Travel By:

A Top Priority For Me On This Trip:

Any Layovers Or Detours On This Trip?

I Want To Experience:

If Yes To The Previous Prompt, Where And Why?

Will I Have An Itinerary For This Trip Or Will I Just Freestyle My Visit?

Why Does This Trip Matter To Me?

I Plan To Learn:

Trip Name:

Location: Arrival Date: Arrival Time: End Of Trip Date:

During This Trip, I Felt: Best Memory Of The Trip:

Foods And Drinks I Enjoyed: I Am Now Inspired To:

Places I Have Visited: What I Would Recommend/Not Recommend About This Trip:

What I Enjoyed During My Trip: Would I Come Here Again?

What I Did Not Enjoy During My Trip: I Realized:

I Met:

My Trip Story:

Attach Picture

Some Places Feel Like Home.

I Know
I Can
Conquer
The
World.

Off To My Next Adventure

Date: My Level Of Excitement: 😊 😄 😵 😨

I Am Naming This Trip:

Where Am I Going?

Who Am I Going With?

How Long Is This Trip?

I Plan To Travel By:

Any Layovers Or Detours On This Trip?

If Yes To The Previous Prompt, Where And Why?

Why Does This Trip Matter To Me?

Where Will I Be Staying?

The Reason For This Trip:

My Trip Budget:

I Want To See:

A Top Priority For Me On This Trip:

I Want To Experience:

Will I Have An Itinerary For This Trip Or Will I Just Freestyle My Visit?

I Plan To Learn:

Trip Name:

Location: Arrival Date: Arrival Time: End Of Trip Date:

During This Trip, I Felt: Best Memory Of The Trip:

Foods And Drinks I Enjoyed: I Am Now Inspired To:

Places I Have Visited: What I Would Recommend/Not Recommend About This Trip:

What I Enjoyed During My Trip: Would I Come Here Again?

What I Did Not Enjoy During My Trip: I Realized:

I Met:

Attach Picture

My Trip Story:

Off To My Next Adventure

Date: _____ My Level Of Excitement:

I Am Naming This Trip:

Where Will I Be Staying?

Where Am I Going?

The Reason For This Trip:

Who Am I Going With?

My Trip Budget:

How Long Is This Trip?

I Want To See:

I Plan To Travel By:

A Top Priority For Me On This Trip:

Any Layovers Or Detours On This Trip?

I Want To Experience:

If Yes To The Previous Prompt, Where And Why?

Will I Have An Itinerary For This Trip Or Will I Just Freestyle My Visit?

Why Does This Trip Matter To Me?

I Plan To Learn:

Trip Name:

Location: Arrival Date: Arrival Time: End Of Trip Date:

During This Trip, I Felt: | Best Memory Of The Trip:

Foods And Drinks I Enjoyed: | I Am Now Inspired To:

Places I Have Visited: | What I Would Recommend/Not
                                  | Recommend About This Trip:

What I Enjoyed During My Trip: | Would I Come Here Again?

What I Did Not Enjoy During My Trip: | I Realized:

I Met:

My Trip Story:

Attach Picture

My Road Trip Playlist....

Traveling Sets My Spirit Free.

Off To My Next Adventure

Date: _____ My Level Of Excitement:

I Am Naming This Trip:

Where Will I Be Staying?

Where Am I Going?

The Reason For This Trip:

Who Am I Going With?

My Trip Budget:

How Long Is This Trip?

I Want To See:

I Plan To Travel By:

A Top Priority For Me On This Trip:

Any Layovers Or Detours On This Trip?

I Want To Experience:

If Yes To The Previous Prompt, Where And Why?

Will I Have An Itinerary For This Trip Or Will I Just Freestyle My Visit?

Why Does This Trip Matter To Me?

I Plan To Learn:

Trip Name:

Location: Arrival Date: Arrival Time: End Of Trip Date:

During This Trip, I Felt: Best Memory Of The Trip:

Foods And Drinks I Enjoyed: I Am Now Inspired To:

Places I Have Visited: What I Would Recommend/Not
                                Recommend About This Trip:

What I Enjoyed During My Trip: Would I Come Here Again?

What I Did Not Enjoy During My Trip: I Realized:

I Met:

Attach Picture

My Trip Story:

Leaving My Comfort Zone.

Eat. Sleep.

Love.

Travel.

Repeat.

Off To My Next Adventure

Date: _____   My Level Of Excitement: 😍 😁 🥳 😱

I Am Naming This Trip:

Where Am I Going?

Who Am I Going With?

How Long Is This Trip?

I Plan To Travel By:

Any Layovers Or Detours On This Trip?

If Yes To The Previous Prompt, Where And Why?

Why Does This Trip Matter To Me?

Where Will I Be Staying?

The Reason For This Trip:

My Trip Budget:

I Want To See:

A Top Priority For Me On This Trip:

I Want To Experience:

Will I Have An Itinerary For This Trip Or Will I Just Freestyle My Visit?

I Plan To Learn:

Trip Name:

Location: Arrival Date: Arrival Time: End Of Trip Date:

During This Trip, I Felt:

Best Memory Of The Trip:

Foods And Drinks I Enjoyed:

I Am Now Inspired To:

Places I Have Visited:

What I Would Recommend/Not Recommend About This Trip:

What I Enjoyed During My Trip:

Would I Come Here Again?

What I Did Not Enjoy During My Trip:

I Realized:

I Met:

Attach Picture

My Trip Story:

Off To My Next Adventure

Date: _____   My Level Of Excitement: 😊 😁 😖 😨

I Am Naming This Trip:

Where Am I Going?

Who Am I Going With?

How Long Is This Trip?

I Plan To Travel By:

Any Layovers Or Detours On This Trip?

If Yes To The Previous Prompt, Where And Why?

Why Does This Trip Matter To Me?

Where Will I Be Staying?

The Reason For This Trip:

My Trip Budget:

I Want To See:

A Top Priority For Me On This Trip:

I Want To Experience:

Will I Have An Itinerary For This Trip Or Will I Just Freestyle My Visit?

I Plan To Learn:

Trip Name:

Location: Arrival Date: Arrival Time: End Of Trip Date:

During This Trip, I Felt: Best Memory Of The Trip:

Foods And Drinks I Enjoyed: I Am Now Inspired To:

Places I Have Visited: What I Would Recommend/Not
                                  Recommend About This Trip:

What I Enjoyed During My Trip: Would I Come Here Again?

What I Did Not Enjoy During My Trip: I Realized:

I Met:

Attach Picture

My Trip Story:

God Has Shown Me....

Leaving The Daily Routine Behind.

Off To My Next Adventure

Date: _____ My Level Of Excitement: 😍 😄 😋 🥶

I Am Naming This Trip:

Where Am I Going?

Who Am I Going With?

How Long Is This Trip?

I Plan To Travel By:

Any Layovers Or Detours On This Trip?

If Yes To The Previous Prompt, Where And Why?

Why Does This Trip Matter To Me?

Where Will I Be Staying?

The Reason For This Trip:

My Trip Budget:

I Want To See:

A Top Priority For Me On This Trip:

I Want To Experience:

Will I Have An Itinerary For This Trip Or Will I Just Freestyle My Visit?

I Plan To Learn:

Trip Name:

Location: Arrival Date: Arrival Time: End Of Trip Date:

During This Trip, I Felt: Best Memory Of The Trip:

Foods And Drinks I Enjoyed: I Am Now Inspired To:

Places I Have Visited: What I Would Recommend/Not
                                             Recommend About This Trip:

What I Enjoyed During My Trip: Would I Come Here Again?

What I Did Not Enjoy During My Trip: I Realized:

I Met:

Attach Picture

My Trip Story:

Off To My Next Adventure

Date: _____ My Level Of Excitement: 😍 😁 🥹 😱

I Am Naming This Trip:

Where Will I Be Staying?

Where Am I Going?

The Reason For This Trip:

Who Am I Going With?

My Trip Budget:

How Long Is This Trip?

I Want To See:

I Plan To Travel By:

A Top Priority For Me On This Trip:

Any Layovers Or Detours On This Trip?

I Want To Experience:

If Yes To The Previous Prompt, Where And Why?

Will I Have An Itinerary For This Trip Or Will I Just Freestyle My Visit?

Why Does This Trip Matter To Me?

I Plan To Learn:

Trip Name:

Location: Arrival Date: Arrival Time: End Of Trip Date:

During This Trip, I Felt: Best Memory Of The Trip:

Foods And Drinks I Enjoyed: I Am Now Inspired To:

Places I Have Visited: What I Would Recommend/Not Recommend About This Trip:

What I Enjoyed During My Trip: Would I Come Here Again?

What I Did Not Enjoy During My Trip: I Realized:

I Met:

My Trip Story:

Attach Picture

Traveling Will Be My New Normal.

My Passport Tells A Story.

Off To My Next Adventure

Date: _____   My Level Of Excitement:

I Am Naming This Trip:	Where Will I Be Staying?
Where Am I Going?	The Reason For This Trip:
Who Am I Going With?	My Trip Budget:
How Long Is This Trip?	I Want To See:
I Plan To Travel By:	A Top Priority For Me On This Trip:
Any Layovers Or Detours On This Trip?	I Want To Experience:
If Yes To The Previous Prompt, Where And Why?	Will I Have An Itinerary For This Trip Or Will I Just Freestyle My Visit?
Why Does This Trip Matter To Me?	I Plan To Learn:

Trip Name:

Location: Arrival Date: Arrival Time: End Of Trip Date:

During This Trip, I Felt: Best Memory Of The Trip:

Foods And Drinks I Enjoyed: I Am Now Inspired To:

Places I Have Visited: What I Would Recommend/Not
                                          Recommend About This Trip:

What I Enjoyed During My Trip: Would I Come Here Again?

What I Did Not Enjoy During My Trip: I Realized:

I Met:

My Trip Story:

Attach Picture

Off To My Next Adventure

Date: _____ My Level Of Excitement:

I Am Naming This Trip:	Where Will I Be Staying?
Where Am I Going?	The Reason For This Trip:
Who Am I Going With?	My Trip Budget:
How Long Is This Trip?	I Want To See:
I Plan To Travel By:	A Top Priority For Me On This Trip:
Any Layovers Or Detours On This Trip?	I Want To Experience:
If Yes To The Previous Prompt, Where And Why?	Will I Have An Itinerary For This Trip Or Will I Just Freestyle My Visit?
Why Does This Trip Matter To Me?	I Plan To Learn:

Trip Name:

Location: Arrival Date: Arrival Time: End Of Trip Date:

During This Trip, I Felt:

Best Memory Of The Trip:

Foods And Drinks I Enjoyed:

I Am Now Inspired To:

Places I Have Visited:

What I Would Recommend/Not Recommend About This Trip:

What I Enjoyed During My Trip:

Would I Come Here Again?

What I Did Not Enjoy During My Trip:

I Realized:

I Met:

My Trip Story:

Attach Picture

What I Love About The World....

I Like To Collect....

I Am Saying Yes To New Adventures.

I Am

Choosing To

Make My

Soul Happy.

Off To My Next Adventure

Date: My Level Of Excitement:

I Am Naming This Trip:

Where Will I Be Staying?

Where Am I Going?

The Reason For This Trip:

Who Am I Going With?

My Trip Budget:

How Long Is This Trip?

I Want To See:

I Plan To Travel By:

A Top Priority For Me On This Trip:

Any Layovers Or Detours On This Trip?

I Want To Experience:

If Yes To The Previous Prompt, Where And Why?

Will I Have An Itinerary For This Trip Or Will I Just Freestyle My Visit?

Why Does This Trip Matter To Me?

I Plan To Learn:

Trip Name:

Location: Arrival Date: Arrival Time: End Of Trip Date:

During This Trip, I Felt: Best Memory Of The Trip:

Foods And Drinks I Enjoyed: I Am Now Inspired To:

Places I Have Visited: What I Would Recommend/Not
                                             Recommend About This Trip:

Attach Picture

What I Enjoyed During My Trip: Would I Come Here Again?

What I Did Not Enjoy During My Trip: I Realized:

I Met:

My Trip Story:

Off To My Next Adventure

Date: _____ My Level Of Excitement:

I Am Naming This Trip:

Where Am I Going?

Who Am I Going With?

How Long Is This Trip?

I Plan To Travel By:

Any Layovers Or Detours On This Trip?

If Yes To The Previous Prompt, Where And Why?

Why Does This Trip Matter To Me?

Where Will I Be Staying?

The Reason For This Trip:

My Trip Budget:

I Want To See:

A Top Priority For Me On This Trip:

I Want To Experience:

Will I Have An Itinerary For This Trip Or Will I Just Freestyle My Visit?

I Plan To Learn:

Trip Name:

Location: Arrival Date: Arrival Time: End Of Trip Date:

During This Trip, I Felt: Best Memory Of The Trip:

Foods And Drinks I Enjoyed: I Am Now Inspired To:

Places I Have Visited: What I Would Recommend/Not
                                        Recommend About This Trip:

What I Enjoyed During My Trip: Would I Come Here Again?

What I Did Not Enjoy During My Trip: I Realized:

I Met:

My Trip Story:

Attach Picture

Off To My Next Adventure

Date: _____   My Level Of Excitement: 😍 😄 😣 😱

I Am Naming This Trip:

Where Will I Be Staying?

Where Am I Going?

The Reason For This Trip:

Who Am I Going With?

My Trip Budget:

How Long Is This Trip?

I Want To See:

I Plan To Travel By:

A Top Priority For Me On This Trip:

Any Layovers Or Detours On This Trip?

I Want To Experience:

If Yes To The Previous Prompt, Where And Why?

Will I Have An Itinerary For This Trip Or Will I Just Freestyle My Visit?

Why Does This Trip Matter To Me?

I Plan To Learn:

Trip Name:

Location: Arrival Date: Arrival Time: End Of Trip Date:

During This Trip, I Felt: Best Memory Of The Trip:

Foods And Drinks I Enjoyed: I Am Now Inspired To:

Places I Have Visited: What I Would Recommend/Not
                                          Recommend About This Trip:

What I Enjoyed During My Trip: Would I Come Here Again?

What I Did Not Enjoy During My Trip: I Realized:

I Met:

My Trip Story:

Attach Picture

New Foods I Have Tasted And Loved From My Travels....

I Do The Things I Love.

Off To My Next Adventure

Date: _____ My Level Of Excitement:

I Am Naming This Trip:

Where Am I Going?

Who Am I Going With?

How Long Is This Trip?

I Plan To Travel By:

Any Layovers Or Detours On This Trip?

If Yes To The Previous Prompt, Where And Why?

Why Does This Trip Matter To Me?

Where Will I Be Staying?

The Reason For This Trip:

My Trip Budget:

I Want To See:

A Top Priority For Me On This Trip:

I Want To Experience:

Will I Have An Itinerary For This Trip Or Will I Just Freestyle My Visit?

I Plan To Learn:

Trip Name:

Location: Arrival Date: Arrival Time: End Of Trip Date:

During This Trip, I Felt: Best Memory Of The Trip:

Foods And Drinks I Enjoyed: I Am Now Inspired To:

Places I Have Visited: What I Would Recommend/Not
                                          Recommend About This Trip:

What I Enjoyed During My Trip: Would I Come Here Again?

What I Did Not Enjoy During My Trip: I Realized:

I Met:

My Trip Story:

Attach Picture

Off To My Next Adventure

Date: _____   My Level Of Excitement:

I Am Naming This Trip:

Where Am I Going?

Who Am I Going With?

How Long Is This Trip?

I Plan To Travel By:

Any Layovers Or Detours On This Trip?

If Yes To The Previous Prompt, Where And Why?

Why Does This Trip Matter To Me?

Where Will I Be Staying?

The Reason For This Trip:

My Trip Budget:

I Want To See:

A Top Priority For Me On This Trip:

I Want To Experience:

Will I Have An Itinerary For This Trip Or Will I Just Freestyle My Visit?

I Plan To Learn:

Trip Name:

Location: Arrival Date: Arrival Time: End Of Trip Date:

During This Trip, I Felt: Best Memory Of The Trip:

Foods And Drinks I Enjoyed: I Am Now Inspired To:

Places I Have Visited: What I Would Recommend/Not Recommend About This Trip:

What I Enjoyed During My Trip: Would I Come Here Again?

What I Did Not Enjoy During My Trip: I Realized:

I Met:

Attach Picture

My Trip Story:

Love Travels Far And Still Finds Its Way Home.

I Travel To Learn.

Off To My Next Adventure

Date: _____   My Level Of Excitement:

I Am Naming This Trip:

Where Will I Be Staying?

Where Am I Going?

The Reason For This Trip:

Who Am I Going With?

My Trip Budget:

How Long Is This Trip?

I Want To See:

I Plan To Travel By:

A Top Priority For Me On This Trip:

Any Layovers Or Detours On This Trip?

I Want To Experience:

If Yes To The Previous Prompt, Where And Why?

Will I Have An Itinerary For This Trip Or Will I Just Freestyle My Visit?

Why Does This Trip Matter To Me?

I Plan To Learn:

Trip Name:

Location: Arrival Date: Arrival Time: End Of Trip Date:

During This Trip, I Felt: Best Memory Of The Trip:

Foods And Drinks I Enjoyed: I Am Now Inspired To:

Places I Have Visited: What I Would Recommend/Not Recommend About This Trip:

What I Enjoyed During My Trip: Would I Come Here Again?

What I Did Not Enjoy During My Trip: I Realized:

I Met:

My Trip Story:

Attach Picture

Off To My Next Adventure

Date: _____   My Level Of Excitement: 😍 😄 🥰 😲

I Am Naming This Trip:

Where Will I Be Staying?

Where Am I Going?

The Reason For This Trip:

Who Am I Going With?

My Trip Budget:

How Long Is This Trip?

I Want To See:

I Plan To Travel By:

A Top Priority For Me On This Trip:

Any Layovers Or Detours On This Trip?

I Want To Experience:

If Yes To The Previous Prompt, Where And Why?

Will I Have An Itinerary For This Trip Or Will I Just Freestyle My Visit?

Why Does This Trip Matter To Me?

I Plan To Learn:

Trip Name:

Location: Arrival Date: Arrival Time: End Of Trip Date:

During This Trip, I Felt:

Best Memory Of The Trip:

Foods And Drinks I Enjoyed:

I Am Now Inspired To:

Places I Have Visited:

What I Would Recommend/Not Recommend About This Trip:

What I Enjoyed During My Trip:

Would I Come Here Again?

What I Did Not Enjoy During My Trip:

I Realized:

I Met:

Attach Picture

My Trip Story:

Off To My Next Adventure

Date: My Level Of Excitement:

I Am Naming This Trip:

Where Am I Going?

Who Am I Going With?

How Long Is This Trip?

I Plan To Travel By:

Any Layovers Or Detours On This Trip?

If Yes To The Previous Prompt, Where And Why?

Why Does This Trip Matter To Me?

Where Will I Be Staying?

The Reason For This Trip:

My Trip Budget:

I Want To See:

A Top Priority For Me On This Trip:

I Want To Experience:

Will I Have An Itinerary For This Trip Or Will I Just Freestyle My Visit?

I Plan To Learn:

Trip Name:

Location: Arrival Date: Arrival Time: End Of Trip Date:

During This Trip, I Felt: Best Memory Of The Trip:

Foods And Drinks I Enjoyed: I Am Now Inspired To:

Places I Have Visited: What I Would Recommend/Not
                                     Recommend About This Trip:

What I Enjoyed During My Trip: Would I Come Here Again?

What I Did Not Enjoy During My Trip: I Realized:

I Met:

Attach Picture

My Trip Story:

By
Traveling
I Conquer
Myself.

I Laugh In France, London, Tokyo, Chicago, Montreal, Haiti, And Brazil.

Off To My Next Adventure

Date: My Level Of Excitement:

I Am Naming This Trip:

Where Will I Be Staying?

Where Am I Going?

The Reason For This Trip:

Who Am I Going With?

My Trip Budget:

How Long Is This Trip?

I Want To See:

I Plan To Travel By:

A Top Priority For Me On This Trip:

Any Layovers Or Detours On This Trip?

I Want To Experience:

If Yes To The Previous Prompt, Where And Why?

Will I Have An Itinerary For This Trip Or Will I Just Freestyle My Visit?

Why Does This Trip Matter To Me?

I Plan To Learn:

126

Trip Name:

Location: Arrival Date: Arrival Time: End Of Trip Date:

During This Trip, I Felt:

Best Memory Of The Trip:

Foods And Drinks I Enjoyed:

I Am Now Inspired To:

Places I Have Visited:

What I Would Recommend/Not Recommend About This Trip:

What I Enjoyed During My Trip:

Would I Come Here Again?

What I Did Not Enjoy During My Trip:

I Realized:

I Met:

Attach Picture

My Trip Story:

Off To My Next Adventure

Date: My Level Of Excitement:

I Am Naming This Trip:

Where Will I Be Staying?

Where Am I Going?

The Reason For This Trip:

Who Am I Going With?

My Trip Budget:

How Long Is This Trip?

I Want To See:

I Plan To Travel By:

A Top Priority For Me On This Trip:

Any Layovers Or Detours On This Trip?

I Want To Experience:

If Yes To The Previous Prompt, Where And Why?

Will I Have An Itinerary For This Trip Or Will I Just Freestyle My Visit?

Why Does This Trip Matter To Me?

I Plan To Learn:

Trip Name:

Location: Arrival Date: Arrival Time: End Of Trip Date:

During This Trip, I Felt: Best Memory Of The Trip:

Foods And Drinks I Enjoyed: I Am Now Inspired To:

Places I Have Visited: What I Would Recommend/Not
                                           Recommend About This Trip:

What I Enjoyed During My Trip: Would I Come Here Again?

What I Did Not Enjoy During My Trip: I Realized:

I Met:

My Trip Story:

Attach Picture

Off To My Next Adventure

Date: _____ My Level Of Excitement: 😍 😄 😥 😱

I Am Naming This Trip:

Where Am I Going?

Who Am I Going With?

How Long Is This Trip?

I Plan To Travel By:

Any Layovers Or Detours On This Trip?

If Yes To The Previous Prompt, Where And Why?

Why Does This Trip Matter To Me?

Where Will I Be Staying?

The Reason For This Trip:

My Trip Budget:

I Want To See:

A Top Priority For Me On This Trip:

I Want To Experience:

Will I Have An Itinerary For This Trip Or Will I Just Freestyle My Visit?

I Plan To Learn:

Trip Name:

Location: Arrival Date: Arrival Time: End Of Trip Date:

During This Trip, I Felt: Best Memory Of The Trip:

Foods And Drinks I Enjoyed: I Am Now Inspired To:

Places I Have Visited: What I Would Recommend/Not
                                       Recommend About This Trip:

What I Enjoyed During My Trip: Would I Come Here Again?

What I Did Not Enjoy During My Trip: I Realized:

I Met:

Attach Picture

My Trip Story:

131

Tickets I Have Collected From My Travels....

I Discover Pieces Of Myself In Different Parts Of The World.

Off To My Next Adventure

Date: _____ My Level Of Excitement: 😍 😄 😏 😨

I Am Naming This Trip:

Where Will I Be Staying?

Where Am I Going?

The Reason For This Trip:

Who Am I Going With?

My Trip Budget:

How Long Is This Trip?

I Want To See:

I Plan To Travel By:

A Top Priority For Me On This Trip:

Any Layovers Or Detours On This Trip?

I Want To Experience:

If Yes To The Previous Prompt, Where And Why?

Will I Have An Itinerary For This Trip Or Will I Just Freestyle My Visit?

Why Does This Trip Matter To Me?

I Plan To Learn:

Trip Name:

Location: Arrival Date: Arrival Time: End Of Trip Date:

During This Trip, I Felt: Best Memory Of The Trip:

Foods And Drinks I Enjoyed: I Am Now Inspired To:

Places I Have Visited: What I Would Recommend/Not
                                        Recommend About This Trip:

What I Enjoyed During My Trip: Would I Come Here Again?

What I Did Not Enjoy During My Trip: I Realized:

I Met:

My Trip Story:

Attach Picture

Off To My Next Adventure

Date: _____ My Level Of Excitement:

I Am Naming This Trip:

Where Will I Be Staying?

Where Am I Going?

The Reason For This Trip:

Who Am I Going With?

My Trip Budget:

How Long Is This Trip?

I Want To See:

I Plan To Travel By:

A Top Priority For Me On This Trip:

Any Layovers Or Detours On This Trip?

I Want To Experience:

If Yes To The Previous Prompt, Where And Why?

Will I Have An Itinerary For This Trip Or Will I Just Freestyle My Visit?

Why Does This Trip Matter To Me?

I Plan To Learn:

Trip Name:

Location: Arrival Date: Arrival Time: End Of Trip Date:

During This Trip, I Felt: Best Memory Of The Trip:

Foods And Drinks I Enjoyed: I Am Now Inspired To:

Places I Have Visited: What I Would Recommend/Not
Recommend About This Trip:

Attach Picture

What I Enjoyed During My Trip: Would I Come Here Again?

What I Did Not Enjoy During My Trip: I Realized:

I Met:

My Trip Story:

Off To My Next Adventure

Date: My Level Of Excitement:

I Am Naming This Trip:

Where Will I Be Staying?

Where Am I Going?

The Reason For This Trip:

Who Am I Going With?

My Trip Budget:

How Long Is This Trip?

I Want To See:

I Plan To Travel By:

A Top Priority For Me On This Trip:

Any Layovers Or Detours On This Trip?

I Want To Experience:

If Yes To The Previous Prompt, Where And Why?

Will I Have An Itinerary For This Trip Or Will I Just Freestyle My Visit?

Why Does This Trip Matter To Me?

I Plan To Learn:

Trip Name:

Location: Arrival Date: Arrival Time: End Of Trip Date:

During This Trip, I Felt: Best Memory Of The Trip:

Foods And Drinks I Enjoyed: I Am Now Inspired To:

Places I Have Visited: What I Would Recommend/Not
                                          Recommend About This Trip:

What I Enjoyed During My Trip: Would I Come Here Again?

What I Did Not Enjoy During My Trip: I Realized:

I Met:

My Trip Story:

Attach Picture

Everywhere I Go, I See The Beauty Of God.

My Travel Notes

Off To My Next Adventure

Date: _____ My Level Of Excitement:

I Am Naming This Trip:

Where Will I Be Staying?

Where Am I Going?

The Reason For This Trip:

Who Am I Going With?

My Trip Budget:

How Long Is This Trip?

I Want To See:

I Plan To Travel By:

A Top Priority For Me On This Trip:

Any Layovers Or Detours On This Trip?

I Want To Experience:

If Yes To The Previous Prompt, Where And Why?

Will I Have An Itinerary For This Trip Or Will I Just Freestyle My Visit?

Why Does This Trip Matter To Me?

I Plan To Learn:

Trip Name:

Location: Arrival Date: Arrival Time: End Of Trip Date:

During This Trip, I Felt: Best Memory Of The Trip:

Foods And Drinks I Enjoyed: I Am Now Inspired To:

Places I Have Visited: What I Would Recommend/Not Recommend About This Trip:

What I Enjoyed During My Trip: Would I Come Here Again?

What I Did Not Enjoy During My Trip: I Realized:

I Met:

My Trip Story:

Attach Picture

Off To My Next Adventure

Date: _____ My Level Of Excitement: 😍 😄 😕 😱

I Am Naming This Trip:

Where Am I Going?

Who Am I Going With?

How Long Is This Trip?

I Plan To Travel By:

Any Layovers Or Detours On This Trip?

If Yes To The Previous Prompt, Where And Why?

Why Does This Trip Matter To Me?

Where Will I Be Staying?

The Reason For This Trip:

My Trip Budget:

I Want To See:

A Top Priority For Me On This Trip:

I Want To Experience:

Will I Have An Itinerary For This Trip Or Will I Just Freestyle My Visit?

I Plan To Learn:

Trip Name:

Location: Arrival Date: Arrival Time: End Of Trip Date:

During This Trip, I Felt: Best Memory Of The Trip:

Foods And Drinks I Enjoyed: I Am Now Inspired To:

Places I Have Visited: What I Would Recommend/Not
                                Recommend About This Trip:

What I Enjoyed During My Trip: Would I Come Here Again?

What I Did Not Enjoy During My Trip: I Realized:

I Met:

Attach Picture

My Trip Story:

The Best Conversation I Have Had From All My Travel Adventures....

Feeling Good

Living Better.

Off To My Next Adventure

Date: My Level Of Excitement:

I Am Naming This Trip:

Where Will I Be Staying?

Where Am I Going?

The Reason For This Trip:

Who Am I Going With?

My Trip Budget:

How Long Is This Trip?

I Want To See:

I Plan To Travel By:

A Top Priority For Me On This Trip:

Any Layovers Or Detours On This Trip?

I Want To Experience:

If Yes To The Previous Prompt, Where And Why?

Will I Have An Itinerary For This Trip Or Will I Just Freestyle My Visit?

Why Does This Trip Matter To Me?

I Plan To Learn:

Trip Name:

Location: Arrival Date: Arrival Time: End Of Trip Date:

During This Trip, I Felt: Best Memory Of The Trip:

Foods And Drinks I Enjoyed: I Am Now Inspired To:

Places I Have Visited: What I Would Recommend/Not
                                             Recommend About This Trip:

What I Enjoyed During My Trip: Would I Come Here Again?

What I Did Not Enjoy During My Trip: I Realized:

I Met:

My Trip Story:

Attach Picture

Off To My Next Adventure

Date: My Level Of Excitement: 😍 😁 😌 😰

I Am Naming This Trip:

Where Am I Going?

Who Am I Going With?

How Long Is This Trip?

I Plan To Travel By:

Any Layovers Or Detours On This Trip?

If Yes To The Previous Prompt, Where And Why?

Why Does This Trip Matter To Me?

Where Will I Be Staying?

The Reason For This Trip:

My Trip Budget:

I Want To See:

A Top Priority For Me On This Trip:

I Want To Experience:

Will I Have An Itinerary For This Trip Or Will I Just Freestyle My Visit?

I Plan To Learn:

Trip Name:

Location: Arrival Date: Arrival Time: End Of Trip Date:

During This Trip, I Felt: Best Memory Of The Trip:

Foods And Drinks I Enjoyed: I Am Now Inspired To:

Places I Have Visited: What I Would Recommend/Not
                                           Recommend About This Trip:

What I Enjoyed During My Trip: Would I Come Here Again?

What I Did Not Enjoy During My Trip: I Realized:

I Met:

Attach Picture

My Trip Story:

Some Detours I Have Made....

Some Of My Best Souvenirs Are
(Write What They Are And
Where They Are From)....

Off To My Next Adventure

Date: _____   My Level Of Excitement: 😍   😁   😖   😨

I Am Naming This Trip:

Where Will I Be Staying?

Where Am I Going?

The Reason For This Trip:

Who Am I Going With?

My Trip Budget:

How Long Is This Trip?

I Want To See:

I Plan To Travel By:

A Top Priority For Me On This Trip:

Any Layovers Or Detours On This Trip?

I Want To Experience:

If Yes To The Previous Prompt, Where And Why?

Will I Have An Itinerary For This Trip Or Will I Just Freestyle My Visit?

Why Does This Trip Matter To Me?

I Plan To Learn:

Trip Name:

Location: Arrival Date: Arrival Time: End Of Trip Date:

During This Trip, I Felt: Best Memory Of The Trip:

Foods And Drinks I Enjoyed: I Am Now Inspired To:

Places I Have Visited: What I Would Recommend/Not
                                           Recommend About This Trip:

What I Enjoyed During My Trip: Would I Come Here Again?

What I Did Not Enjoy During My Trip: I Realized:

I Met:

Attach Picture

My Trip Story:

Off To My Next Adventure

Date: _____   My Level Of Excitement: 😍 😁 😅 😱

I Am Naming This Trip:

Where Am I Going?

Who Am I Going With?

How Long Is This Trip?

I Plan To Travel By:

Any Layovers Or Detours On This Trip?

If Yes To The Previous Prompt, Where And Why?

Why Does This Trip Matter To Me?

Where Will I Be Staying?

The Reason For This Trip:

My Trip Budget:

I Want To See:

A Top Priority For Me On This Trip:

I Want To Experience:

Will I Have An Itinerary For This Trip Or Will I Just Freestyle My Visit?

I Plan To Learn:

Trip Name:

Location: Arrival Date: Arrival Time: End Of Trip Date:

During This Trip, I Felt:

Best Memory Of The Trip:

Foods And Drinks I Enjoyed:

I Am Now Inspired To:

Places I Have Visited:

What I Would Recommend/Not Recommend About This Trip:

Attach Picture

What I Enjoyed During My Trip:

Would I Come Here Again?

What I Did Not Enjoy During My Trip:

I Realized:

I Met:

My Trip Story:

Free.

Free.

Free.

I Feel

Free.

Waking Up In Different Time Zones.

Off To My Next Adventure

Date: _____ My Level Of Excitement:

I Am Naming This Trip:

Where Will I Be Staying?

Where Am I Going?

The Reason For This Trip:

Who Am I Going With?

My Trip Budget:

How Long Is This Trip?

I Want To See:

I Plan To Travel By:

A Top Priority For Me On This Trip:

Any Layovers Or Detours On This Trip?

I Want To Experience:

If Yes To The Previous Prompt, Where And Why?

Will I Have An Itinerary For This Trip Or Will I Just Freestyle My Visit?

Why Does This Trip Matter To Me?

I Plan To Learn:

Trip Name:

Location: Arrival Date: Arrival Time: End Of Trip Date:

During This Trip, I Felt: Best Memory Of The Trip:

Foods And Drinks I Enjoyed: I Am Now Inspired To:

Places I Have Visited: What I Would Recommend/Not
                                          Recommend About This Trip:

What I Enjoyed During My Trip: Would I Come Here Again?

What I Did Not Enjoy During My Trip: I Realized:

I Met:

My Trip Story:

Attach Picture

Off To My Next Adventure

Date: _____   My Level Of Excitement:

I Am Naming This Trip:

Where Will I Be Staying?

Where Am I Going?

The Reason For This Trip:

Who Am I Going With?

My Trip Budget:

How Long Is This Trip?

I Want To See:

I Plan To Travel By:

A Top Priority For Me On This Trip:

Any Layovers Or Detours On This Trip?

I Want To Experience:

If Yes To The Previous Prompt, Where And Why?

Will I Have An Itinerary For This Trip Or Will I Just Freestyle My Visit?

Why Does This Trip Matter To Me?

I Plan To Learn:

Trip Name:

Location: Arrival Date: Arrival Time: End Of Trip Date:

During This Trip, I Felt: Best Memory Of The Trip:

Foods And Drinks I Enjoyed: I Am Now Inspired To:

Places I Have Visited: What I Would Recommend/Not Recommend About This Trip:

What I Enjoyed During My Trip: Would I Come Here Again?

What I Did Not Enjoy During My Trip: I Realized:

I Met:

My Trip Story:

Attach Picture

Off To My Next Adventure

Date: My Level Of Excitement:

I Am Naming This Trip:

Where Will I Be Staying?

Where Am I Going?

The Reason For This Trip:

Who Am I Going With?

My Trip Budget:

How Long Is This Trip?

I Want To See:

I Plan To Travel By:

A Top Priority For Me On This Trip:

Any Layovers Or Detours On This Trip?

I Want To Experience:

If Yes To The Previous Prompt, Where And Why?

Will I Have An Itinerary For This Trip Or Will I Just Freestyle My Visit?

Why Does This Trip Matter To Me?

I Plan To Learn:

Trip Name:

Location: Arrival Date: Arrival Time: End Of Trip Date:

During This Trip, I Felt: Best Memory Of The Trip:

Foods And Drinks I Enjoyed: I Am Now Inspired To:

Places I Have Visited: What I Would Recommend/Not
Recommend About This Trip:

What I Enjoyed During My Trip: Would I Come Here Again?

What I Did Not Enjoy During My Trip: I Realized:

I Met:

My Trip Story:

Attach Picture

Language Converter (Write The Word That I Learned In My Language And Convert It In The Language I Have Learned It In)....

Road
Trips Are

Necessary.

Off To My Next Adventure

Date: _____ My Level Of Excitement: 😍 😁 🥲 😱

I Am Naming This Trip:

Where Will I Be Staying?

Where Am I Going?

The Reason For This Trip:

Who Am I Going With?

My Trip Budget:

How Long Is This Trip?

I Want To See:

I Plan To Travel By:

A Top Priority For Me On This Trip:

Any Layovers Or Detours On This Trip?

I Want To Experience:

If Yes To The Previous Prompt, Where And Why?

Will I Have An Itinerary For This Trip Or Will I Just Freestyle My Visit?

Why Does This Trip Matter To Me?

I Plan To Learn:

Trip Name:

Location: Arrival Date: Arrival Time: End Of Trip Date:

During This Trip, I Felt:

Foods And Drinks I Enjoyed:

Places I Have Visited:

What I Enjoyed During My Trip:

What I Did Not Enjoy During My Trip:

I Met:

My Trip Story:

Best Memory Of The Trip:

I Am Now Inspired To:

What I Would Recommend/Not Recommend About This Trip:

Would I Come Here Again?

I Realized:

Attach Picture

Off To My Next Adventure

Date: My Level Of Excitement:

I Am Naming This Trip:

Where Am I Going?

Who Am I Going With?

How Long Is This Trip?

I Plan To Travel By:

Any Layovers Or Detours On This Trip?

If Yes To The Previous Prompt, Where And Why?

Why Does This Trip Matter To Me?

Where Will I Be Staying?

The Reason For This Trip:

My Trip Budget:

I Want To See:

A Top Priority For Me On This Trip:

I Want To Experience:

Will I Have An Itinerary For This Trip Or Will I Just Freestyle My Visit?

I Plan To Learn:

Trip Name:

Location: Arrival Date: Arrival Time: End Of Trip Date:

During This Trip, I Felt: Best Memory Of The Trip:

Foods And Drinks I Enjoyed: I Am Now Inspired To:

Places I Have Visited: What I Would Recommend/Not
                                              Recommend About This Trip:

What I Enjoyed During My Trip: Would I Come Here Again?

What I Did Not Enjoy During My Trip: I Realized:

I Met:

My Trip Story:

Attach Picture

Off To My Next Adventure

Date: _____   My Level Of Excitement:

I Am Naming This Trip:

Where Will I Be Staying?

Where Am I Going?

The Reason For This Trip:

Who Am I Going With?

My Trip Budget:

How Long Is This Trip?

I Want To See:

I Plan To Travel By:

A Top Priority For Me On This Trip:

Any Layovers Or Detours On This Trip?

I Want To Experience:

If Yes To The Previous Prompt, Where And Why?

Will I Have An Itinerary For This Trip Or Will I Just Freestyle My Visit?

Why Does This Trip Matter To Me?

I Plan To Learn:

Trip Name:

Location: Arrival Date: Arrival Time: End Of Trip Date:

During This Trip, I Felt:

Best Memory Of The Trip:

Foods And Drinks I Enjoyed:

I Am Now Inspired To:

Places I Have Visited:

What I Would Recommend/Not Recommend About This Trip:

What I Enjoyed During My Trip:

Would I Come Here Again?

What I Did Not Enjoy During My Trip:

I Realized:

I Met:

Attach Picture

My Trip Story:

I Feel Too Good To Just Stay At Home.

I

Appreciate

The

World.

Off To My Next Adventure

Date: My Level Of Excitement: 😇 😄 😫 😨

I Am Naming This Trip:

Where Will I Be Staying?

Where Am I Going?

The Reason For This Trip:

Who Am I Going With?

My Trip Budget:

How Long Is This Trip?

I Want To See:

I Plan To Travel By:

A Top Priority For Me On This Trip:

Any Layovers Or Detours On This Trip?

I Want To Experience:

If Yes To The Previous Prompt, Where And Why?

Will I Have An Itinerary For This Trip Or Will I Just Freestyle My Visit?

Why Does This Trip Matter To Me?

I Plan To Learn:

Trip Name:

Location: Arrival Date: Arrival Time: End Of Trip Date:

During This Trip, I Felt:

Best Memory Of The Trip:

Foods And Drinks I Enjoyed:

I Am Now Inspired To:

Places I Have Visited:

What I Would Recommend/Not Recommend About This Trip:

Attach Picture

What I Enjoyed During My Trip:

Would I Come Here Again?

What I Did Not Enjoy During My Trip:

I Realized:

I Met:

My Trip Story:

Off To My Next Adventure

Date: My Level Of Excitement:

I Am Naming This Trip:

Where Will I Be Staying?

Where Am I Going?

The Reason For This Trip:

Who Am I Going With?

My Trip Budget:

How Long Is This Trip?

I Want To See:

I Plan To Travel By:

A Top Priority For Me On This Trip:

Any Layovers Or Detours On This Trip?

I Want To Experience:

If Yes To The Previous Prompt, Where And Why?

Will I Have An Itinerary For This Trip Or Will I Just Freestyle My Visit?

Why Does This Trip Matter To Me?

I Plan To Learn:

Trip Name:

Location: Arrival Date: Arrival Time: End Of Trip Date:

During This Trip, I Felt: Best Memory Of The Trip:

Foods And Drinks I Enjoyed: I Am Now Inspired To:

Places I Have Visited: What I Would Recommend/Not
                                Recommend About This Trip:

What I Enjoyed During My Trip: Would I Come Here Again?

What I Did Not Enjoy During My Trip: I Realized:

I Met:

My Trip Story:

Attach Picture

Off To My Next Adventure

Date: _____ My Level Of Excitement: 😊 😃 😰 😱

I Am Naming This Trip:

Where Am I Going?

Who Am I Going With?

How Long Is This Trip?

I Plan To Travel By:

Any Layovers Or Detours On This Trip?

If Yes To The Previous Prompt, Where And Why?

Why Does This Trip Matter To Me?

Where Will I Be Staying?

The Reason For This Trip:

My Trip Budget:

I Want To See:

A Top Priority For Me On This Trip:

I Want To Experience:

Will I Have An Itinerary For This Trip Or Will I Just Freestyle My Visit?

I Plan To Learn:

Trip Name:

Location: Arrival Date: Arrival Time: End Of Trip Date:

During This Trip, I Felt: Best Memory Of The Trip:

Foods And Drinks I Enjoyed: I Am Now Inspired To:

Places I Have Visited: What I Would Recommend/Not Recommend About This Trip:

Attach Picture

What I Enjoyed During My Trip: Would I Come Here Again?

What I Did Not Enjoy During My Trip: I Realized:

I Met:

My Trip Story:

The Best Travel Advice I Can Give....

Dress Italian,
Drive German,
Kiss French,
Drink Russian,
Party Caribbean,
Spend Arab, Dance
Latin, Dream
American, Speak
Love.

Off To My Next Adventure

Date: _____   My Level Of Excitement:

I Am Naming This Trip:	Where Will I Be Staying?
Where Am I Going?	The Reason For This Trip:
Who Am I Going With?	My Trip Budget:
How Long Is This Trip?	I Want To See:
I Plan To Travel By:	A Top Priority For Me On This Trip:
Any Layovers Or Detours On This Trip?	I Want To Experience:
If Yes To The Previous Prompt, Where And Why?	Will I Have An Itinerary For This Trip Or Will I Just Freestyle My Visit?
Why Does This Trip Matter To Me?	I Plan To Learn:

Trip Name:

Location: Arrival Date: Arrival Time: End Of Trip Date:

During This Trip, I Felt:

Best Memory Of The Trip:

Foods And Drinks I Enjoyed:

I Am Now Inspired To:

Places I Have Visited:

What I Would Recommend/Not Recommend About This Trip:

What I Enjoyed During My Trip:

Would I Come Here Again?

What I Did Not Enjoy During My Trip:

I Realized:

I Met:

Attach Picture

My Trip Story:

Off To My Next Adventure

Date: My Level Of Excitement:

I Am Naming This Trip:

Where Will I Be Staying?

Where Am I Going?

The Reason For This Trip:

Who Am I Going With?

My Trip Budget:

How Long Is This Trip?

I Want To See:

I Plan To Travel By:

A Top Priority For Me On This Trip:

Any Layovers Or Detours On This Trip?

I Want To Experience:

If Yes To The Previous Prompt, Where And Why?

Will I Have An Itinerary For This Trip Or Will I Just Freestyle My Visit?

Why Does This Trip Matter To Me?

I Plan To Learn:

Trip Name:

Location: Arrival Date: Arrival Time: End Of Trip Date:

During This Trip, I Felt: Best Memory Of The Trip:

Foods And Drinks I Enjoyed: I Am Now Inspired To:

Places I Have Visited: What I Would Recommend/Not
                                              Recommend About This Trip:

What I Enjoyed During My Trip: Would I Come Here Again?

What I Did Not Enjoy During My Trip: I Realized:

I Met:

My Trip Story:

Attach Picture

Off To My Next Adventure

Date: _____ My Level Of Excitement:

I Am Naming This Trip:	Where Will I Be Staying?
Where Am I Going?	The Reason For This Trip:
Who Am I Going With?	My Trip Budget:
How Long Is This Trip?	I Want To See:
I Plan To Travel By:	A Top Priority For Me On This Trip:
Any Layovers Or Detours On This Trip?	I Want To Experience:
If Yes To The Previous Prompt, Where And Why?	Will I Have An Itinerary For This Trip Or Will I Just Freestyle My Visit?
Why Does This Trip Matter To Me?	I Plan To Learn:

Trip Name:

Location: Arrival Date: Arrival Time: End Of Trip Date:

During This Trip, I Felt: Best Memory Of The Trip:

Foods And Drinks I Enjoyed: I Am Now Inspired To:

Places I Have Visited: What I Would Recommend/Not Recommend About This Trip:

Attach Picture

What I Enjoyed During My Trip: Would I Come Here Again?

What I Did Not Enjoy During My Trip: I Realized:

I Met:

My Trip Story:

On To The Next Airport.

Just Go.

Off To My Next Adventure

Date: My Level Of Excitement: 😍 😁 😥 😱

I Am Naming This Trip:

Where Will I Be Staying?

Where Am I Going?

The Reason For This Trip:

Who Am I Going With?

My Trip Budget:

How Long Is This Trip?

I Want To See:

I Plan To Travel By:

A Top Priority For Me On This Trip:

Any Layovers Or Detours On This Trip?

I Want To Experience:

If Yes To The Previous Prompt, Where And Why?

Will I Have An Itinerary For This Trip Or Will I Just Freestyle My Visit?

Why Does This Trip Matter To Me?

I Plan To Learn:

Trip Name:

Location: Arrival Date: Arrival Time: End Of Trip Date:

During This Trip, I Felt: Best Memory Of The Trip:

Foods And Drinks I Enjoyed: I Am Now Inspired To:

Places I Have Visited: What I Would Recommend/Not
                                             Recommend About This Trip:

What I Enjoyed During My Trip: Would I Come Here Again?

What I Did Not Enjoy During My Trip: I Realized:

I Met:

Attach Picture

My Trip Story:

Off To My Next Adventure

Date: _____   My Level Of Excitement: 😊 😃 😖 😨

I Am Naming This Trip:

Where Will I Be Staying?

Where Am I Going?

The Reason For This Trip:

Who Am I Going With?

My Trip Budget:

How Long Is This Trip?

I Want To See:

I Plan To Travel By:

A Top Priority For Me On This Trip:

Any Layovers Or Detours On This Trip?

I Want To Experience:

If Yes To The Previous Prompt, Where And Why?

Will I Have An Itinerary For This Trip Or Will I Just Freestyle My Visit?

Why Does This Trip Matter To Me?

I Plan To Learn:

Trip Name:

Location: Arrival Date: Arrival Time: End Of Trip Date:

During This Trip, I Felt: Best Memory Of The Trip:

Foods And Drinks I Enjoyed: I Am Now Inspired To:

Places I Have Visited: What I Would Recommend/Not
                                          Recommend About This Trip:

What I Enjoyed During My Trip: Would I Come Here Again?

What I Did Not Enjoy During My Trip: I Realized:

I Met:

Attach Picture

My Trip Story:

Off To My Next Adventure

Date: My Level Of Excitement:

I Am Naming This Trip:

Where Will I Be Staying?

Where Am I Going?

The Reason For This Trip:

Who Am I Going With?

My Trip Budget:

How Long Is This Trip?

I Want To See:

I Plan To Travel By:

A Top Priority For Me On This Trip:

Any Layovers Or Detours On This Trip?

I Want To Experience:

If Yes To The Previous Prompt, Where And Why?

Will I Have An Itinerary For This Trip Or Will I Just Freestyle My Visit?

Why Does This Trip Matter To Me?

I Plan To Learn:

Trip Name:

Location: Arrival Date: Arrival Time: End Of Trip Date:

During This Trip, I Felt: Best Memory Of The Trip:

Foods And Drinks I Enjoyed: I Am Now Inspired To:

Places I Have Visited: What I Would Recommend/Not
                                             Recommend About This Trip:

What I Enjoyed During My Trip: Would I Come Here Again?

What I Did Not Enjoy During My Trip: I Realized:

I Met:

Attach Picture

My Trip Story:

My Future Trip Ideas....

I Want To See It For Myself.

Off To My Next Adventure

Date: _____   My Level Of Excitement:

I Am Naming This Trip:	Where Will I Be Staying?
Where Am I Going?	The Reason For This Trip:
Who Am I Going With?	My Trip Budget:
How Long Is This Trip?	I Want To See:
I Plan To Travel By:	A Top Priority For Me On This Trip:
Any Layovers Or Detours On This Trip?	I Want To Experience:
If Yes To The Previous Prompt, Where And Why?	Will I Have An Itinerary For This Trip Or Will I Just Freestyle My Visit?
Why Does This Trip Matter To Me?	I Plan To Learn:

Trip Name:

Location: Arrival Date: Arrival Time: End Of Trip Date:

During This Trip, I Felt: Best Memory Of The Trip:

Foods And Drinks I Enjoyed: I Am Now Inspired To:

Places I Have Visited: What I Would Recommend/Not
                                          Recommend About This Trip:

What I Enjoyed During My Trip: Would I Come Here Again?

What I Did Not Enjoy During My Trip: I Realized:

I Met:

Attach Picture

My Trip Story:

Off To My Next Adventure

Date: _____   My Level Of Excitement: 😍   😄   😵   😱

I Am Naming This Trip:

Where Will I Be Staying?

Where Am I Going?

The Reason For This Trip:

Who Am I Going With?

My Trip Budget:

How Long Is This Trip?

I Want To See:

I Plan To Travel By:

A Top Priority For Me On This Trip:

Any Layovers Or Detours On This Trip?

I Want To Experience:

If Yes To The Previous Prompt, Where And Why?

Will I Have An Itinerary For This Trip Or Will I Just Freestyle My Visit?

Why Does This Trip Matter To Me?

I Plan To Learn:

Trip Name:

Location: Arrival Date: Arrival Time: End Of Trip Date:

During This Trip, I Felt: Best Memory Of The Trip:

Foods And Drinks I Enjoyed: I Am Now Inspired To:

Places I Have Visited: What I Would Recommend/Not
                                          Recommend About This Trip:

What I Enjoyed During My Trip: Would I Come Here Again?

What I Did Not Enjoy During My Trip: I Realized:

I Met:

My Trip Story:

Attach Picture

Off To My Next Adventure

Date: _____ My Level Of Excitement: 😍 😄 😖 😱

I Am Naming This Trip:

Where Will I Be Staying?

Where Am I Going?

The Reason For This Trip:

Who Am I Going With?

My Trip Budget:

How Long Is This Trip?

I Want To See:

I Plan To Travel By:

A Top Priority For Me On This Trip:

Any Layovers Or Detours On This Trip?

I Want To Experience:

If Yes To The Previous Prompt, Where And Why?

Will I Have An Itinerary For This Trip Or Will I Just Freestyle My Visit?

Why Does This Trip Matter To Me?

I Plan To Learn:

Trip Name:

Location: Arrival Date: Arrival Time: End Of Trip Date:

During This Trip, I Felt:

Best Memory Of The Trip:

Foods And Drinks I Enjoyed:

I Am Now Inspired To:

Places I Have Visited:

What I Would Recommend/Not Recommend About This Trip:

What I Enjoyed During My Trip:

Would I Come Here Again?

What I Did Not Enjoy During My Trip:

I Realized:

I Met:

Attach Picture

My Trip Story:

Events I Have Traveled To And For....

I Am Going Places.

Off To My Next Adventure

Date: My Level Of Excitement:

I Am Naming This Trip:

Where Will I Be Staying?

Where Am I Going?

The Reason For This Trip:

Who Am I Going With?

My Trip Budget:

How Long Is This Trip?

I Want To See:

I Plan To Travel By:

A Top Priority For Me On This Trip:

Any Layovers Or Detours On This Trip?

I Want To Experience:

If Yes To The Previous Prompt, Where And Why?

Will I Have An Itinerary For This Trip Or Will I Just Freestyle My Visit?

Why Does This Trip Matter To Me?

I Plan To Learn:

Trip Name:

Location: Arrival Date: Arrival Time: End Of Trip Date:

During This Trip, I Felt:

Best Memory Of The Trip:

Foods And Drinks I Enjoyed:

I Am Now Inspired To:

Places I Have Visited:

What I Would Recommend/Not
Recommend About This Trip:

What I Enjoyed During My Trip:

Would I Come Here Again?

What I Did Not Enjoy During My Trip:

I Realized:

I Met:

Attach Picture

My Trip Story:

Off To My Next Adventure

Date: _____   My Level Of Excitement:

I Am Naming This Trip:

Where Am I Going?

Who Am I Going With?

How Long Is This Trip?

I Plan To Travel By:

Any Layovers Or Detours On This Trip?

If Yes To The Previous Prompt, Where And Why?

Why Does This Trip Matter To Me?

Where Will I Be Staying?

The Reason For This Trip:

My Trip Budget:

I Want To See:

A Top Priority For Me On This Trip:

I Want To Experience:

Will I Have An Itinerary For This Trip Or Will I Just Freestyle My Visit?

I Plan To Learn:

Trip Name:

Location: Arrival Date: Arrival Time: End Of Trip Date:

During This Trip, I Felt: Best Memory Of The Trip:

Foods And Drinks I Enjoyed: I Am Now Inspired To:

Places I Have Visited: What I Would Recommend/Not
                                          Recommend About This Trip:

What I Enjoyed During My Trip: Would I Come Here Again?

What I Did Not Enjoy During My Trip: I Realized:

I Met:

Attach Picture

My Trip Story:

Off To My Next Adventure

Date: My Level Of Excitement:

I Am Naming This Trip:

Where Am I Going?

Who Am I Going With?

How Long Is This Trip?

I Plan To Travel By:

Any Layovers Or Detours On This Trip?

If Yes To The Previous Prompt, Where And Why?

Why Does This Trip Matter To Me?

Where Will I Be Staying?

The Reason For This Trip:

My Trip Budget:

I Want To See:

A Top Priority For Me On This Trip:

I Want To Experience:

Will I Have An Itinerary For This Trip Or Will I Just Freestyle My Visit?

I Plan To Learn:

Trip Name:

Location: Arrival Date: Arrival Time: End Of Trip Date:

During This Trip, I Felt: Best Memory Of The Trip:

Foods And Drinks I Enjoyed: I Am Now Inspired To:

Places I Have Visited: What I Would Recommend/Not Recommend About This Trip:

What I Enjoyed During My Trip: Would I Come Here Again?

What I Did Not Enjoy During My Trip: I Realized:

I Met:

My Trip Story:

Attach Picture

When In Doubt, Travel.

When You Travel, Everything Makes Sense.

Off To My Next Adventure

Date: _____   My Level Of Excitement: 😊 😄 😝 😱

I Am Naming This Trip:

Where Am I Going?

Who Am I Going With?

How Long Is This Trip?

I Plan To Travel By:

Any Layovers Or Detours On This Trip?

If Yes To The Previous Prompt, Where And Why?

Why Does This Trip Matter To Me?

Where Will I Be Staying?

The Reason For This Trip:

My Trip Budget:

I Want To See:

A Top Priority For Me On This Trip:

I Want To Experience:

Will I Have An Itinerary For This Trip Or Will I Just Freestyle My Visit?

I Plan To Learn:

Trip Name:

Location: Arrival Date: Arrival Time: End Of Trip Date:

During This Trip, I Felt: Best Memory Of The Trip:

Foods And Drinks I Enjoyed: I Am Now Inspired To:

Places I Have Visited: What I Would Recommend/Not
                                             Recommend About This Trip:

What I Enjoyed During My Trip: Would I Come Here Again?

What I Did Not Enjoy During My Trip: I Realized:

I Met:

Attach Picture

My Trip Story:

Off To My Next Adventure

Date: My Level Of Excitement:

I Am Naming This Trip:

Where Will I Be Staying?

Where Am I Going?

The Reason For This Trip:

Who Am I Going With?

My Trip Budget:

How Long Is This Trip?

I Want To See:

I Plan To Travel By:

A Top Priority For Me On This Trip:

Any Layovers Or Detours On This Trip?

I Want To Experience:

If Yes To The Previous Prompt, Where And Why?

Will I Have An Itinerary For This Trip Or Will I Just Freestyle My Visit?

Why Does This Trip Matter To Me?

I Plan To Learn:

Trip Name:

Location: Arrival Date: Arrival Time: End Of Trip Date:

During This Trip, I Felt: Best Memory Of The Trip:

Foods And Drinks I Enjoyed: I Am Now Inspired To:

Places I Have Visited: What I Would Recommend/Not
Recommend About This Trip:

What I Enjoyed During My Trip: Would I Come Here Again?

What I Did Not Enjoy During My Trip: I Realized:

I Met:

Attach Picture

My Trip Story:

Off To My Next Adventure

Date: My Level Of Excitement:

I Am Naming This Trip:

Where Will I Be Staying?

Where Am I Going?

The Reason For This Trip:

Who Am I Going With?

My Trip Budget:

How Long Is This Trip?

I Want To See:

I Plan To Travel By:

A Top Priority For Me On This Trip:

Any Layovers Or Detours On This Trip?

I Want To Experience:

If Yes To The Previous Prompt, Where And Why?

Will I Have An Itinerary For This Trip Or Will I Just Freestyle My Visit?

Why Does This Trip Matter To Me?

I Plan To Learn:

Trip Name:

Location: Arrival Date: Arrival Time: End Of Trip Date:

During This Trip, I Felt: Best Memory Of The Trip:

Foods And Drinks I Enjoyed: I Am Now Inspired To:

Places I Have Visited: What I Would Recommend/Not
                                           Recommend About This Trip:

What I Enjoyed During My Trip: Would I Come Here Again?

What I Did Not Enjoy During My Trip: I Realized:

I Met:

My Trip Story:

Attach Picture

Hotel Room Numbers I Have Stayed In....

Addresses Of Places I Have Stayed At....

I Am Outta Here.

Off To My Next Adventure

Date: _____ My Level Of Excitement:

I Am Naming This Trip:	Where Will I Be Staying?
Where Am I Going?	The Reason For This Trip:
Who Am I Going With?	My Trip Budget:
How Long Is This Trip?	I Want To See:
I Plan To Travel By:	A Top Priority For Me On This Trip:
Any Layovers Or Detours On This Trip?	I Want To Experience:
If Yes To The Previous Prompt, Where And Why?	Will I Have An Itinerary For This Trip Or Will I Just Freestyle My Visit?
Why Does This Trip Matter To Me?	I Plan To Learn:

Trip Name:

Location: Arrival Date: Arrival Time: End Of Trip Date:

During This Trip, I Felt: Best Memory Of The Trip:

Foods And Drinks I Enjoyed: I Am Now Inspired To:

Places I Have Visited: What I Would Recommend/Not
                                          Recommend About This Trip:

What I Enjoyed During My Trip: Would I Come Here Again?

What I Did Not Enjoy During My Trip: I Realized:

I Met:

Attach Picture

My Trip Story:

Off To My Next Adventure

Date: _____   My Level Of Excitement: ☺ 😄 😕 😱

I Am Naming This Trip:

Where Am I Going?

Who Am I Going With?

How Long Is This Trip?

I Plan To Travel By:

Any Layovers Or Detours On This Trip?

If Yes To The Previous Prompt, Where And Why?

Why Does This Trip Matter To Me?

Where Will I Be Staying?

The Reason For This Trip:

My Trip Budget:

I Want To See:

A Top Priority For Me On This Trip:

I Want To Experience:

Will I Have An Itinerary For This Trip Or Will I Just Freestyle My Visit?

I Plan To Learn:

Trip Name:

Location: Arrival Date: Arrival Time: End Of Trip Date:

During This Trip, I Felt:

Foods And Drinks I Enjoyed:

Places I Have Visited:

What I Enjoyed During My Trip:

What I Did Not Enjoy During My Trip:

I Met:

Best Memory Of The Trip:

I Am Now Inspired To:

What I Would Recommend/Not Recommend About This Trip:

Would I Come Here Again?

I Realized:

Attach Picture

My Trip Story:

227

Off To My Next Adventure

Date: _____   My Level Of Excitement: 😍   😁   😖   😱

I Am Naming This Trip:

Where Am I Going?

Who Am I Going With?

How Long Is This Trip?

I Plan To Travel By:

Any Layovers Or Detours On This Trip?

If Yes To The Previous Prompt, Where And Why?

Why Does This Trip Matter To Me?

Where Will I Be Staying?

The Reason For This Trip:

My Trip Budget:

I Want To See:

A Top Priority For Me On This Trip:

I Want To Experience:

Will I Have An Itinerary For This Trip Or Will I Just Freestyle My Visit?

I Plan To Learn:

Trip Name:

Location: Arrival Date: Arrival Time: End Of Trip Date:

During This Trip, I Felt: Best Memory Of The Trip:

Foods And Drinks I Enjoyed: I Am Now Inspired To:

Places I Have Visited: What I Would Recommend/Not Recommend About This Trip:

What I Enjoyed During My Trip: Would I Come Here Again?

What I Did Not Enjoy During My Trip: I Realized:

I Met:

My Trip Story:

Attach Picture

I Am Out Here Living My Dreams.

I Am Taking Mental Pictures.

Off To My Next Adventure

Date: _____ My Level Of Excitement: 😍 😄 😰 😱

I Am Naming This Trip:

Where Will I Be Staying?

Where Am I Going?

The Reason For This Trip:

Who Am I Going With?

My Trip Budget:

How Long Is This Trip?

I Want To See:

I Plan To Travel By:

A Top Priority For Me On This Trip:

Any Layovers Or Detours On This Trip?

I Want To Experience:

If Yes To The Previous Prompt, Where And Why?

Will I Have An Itinerary For This Trip Or Will I Just Freestyle My Visit?

Why Does This Trip Matter To Me?

I Plan To Learn:

Trip Name:

Location: Arrival Date: Arrival Time: End Of Trip Date:

During This Trip, I Felt: Best Memory Of The Trip:

Foods And Drinks I Enjoyed: I Am Now Inspired To:

Places I Have Visited: What I Would Recommend/Not
                                          Recommend About This Trip:

                                                                              Attach Picture

What I Enjoyed During My Trip: Would I Come Here Again?

What I Did Not Enjoy During My Trip: I Realized:

I Met:

My Trip Story:

Off To My Next Adventure

Date: My Level Of Excitement:

I Am Naming This Trip:

Where Am I Going?

Who Am I Going With?

How Long Is This Trip?

I Plan To Travel By:

Any Layovers Or Detours On This Trip?

If Yes To The Previous Prompt, Where And Why?

Why Does This Trip Matter To Me?

Where Will I Be Staying?

The Reason For This Trip:

My Trip Budget:

I Want To See:

A Top Priority For Me On This Trip:

I Want To Experience:

Will I Have An Itinerary For This Trip Or Will I Just Freestyle My Visit?

I Plan To Learn:

Trip Name:

Location: Arrival Date: Arrival Time: End Of Trip Date:

During This Trip, I Felt: Best Memory Of The Trip:

Foods And Drinks I Enjoyed: I Am Now Inspired To:

Places I Have Visited: What I Would Recommend/Not
                                       Recommend About This Trip:

What I Enjoyed During My Trip: Would I Come Here Again?

What I Did Not Enjoy During My Trip: I Realized:

I Met:

My Trip Story:

Attach Picture

Off To My Next Adventure

Date: My Level Of Excitement:

I Am Naming This Trip:

Where Will I Be Staying?

Where Am I Going?

The Reason For This Trip:

Who Am I Going With?

My Trip Budget:

How Long Is This Trip?

I Want To See:

I Plan To Travel By:

A Top Priority For Me On This Trip:

Any Layovers Or Detours On This Trip?

I Want To Experience:

If Yes To The Previous Prompt, Where And Why?

Will I Have An Itinerary For This Trip Or Will I Just Freestyle My Visit?

Why Does This Trip Matter To Me?

I Plan To Learn:

Trip Name:

Location: Arrival Date: Arrival Time: End Of Trip Date:

During This Trip, I Felt:

Best Memory Of The Trip:

Foods And Drinks I Enjoyed:

I Am Now Inspired To:

Places I Have Visited:

What I Would Recommend/Not Recommend About This Trip:

What I Enjoyed During My Trip:

Would I Come Here Again?

What I Did Not Enjoy During My Trip:

I Realized:

I Met:

Attach Picture

My Trip Story:

The Best Coffees I Have Tasted
Have Come From (Write The
Name And Place)....

The Best Teas I Have Tasted
Have Come From (Write The
Name And Place)....

I Will Not Fear Adventure.

Off To My Next Adventure

Date: _____ My Level Of Excitement:

I Am Naming This Trip:

Where Will I Be Staying?

Where Am I Going?

The Reason For This Trip:

Who Am I Going With?

My Trip Budget:

How Long Is This Trip?

I Want To See:

I Plan To Travel By:

A Top Priority For Me On This Trip:

Any Layovers Or Detours On This Trip?

I Want To Experience:

If Yes To The Previous Prompt, Where And Why?

Will I Have An Itinerary For This Trip Or Will I Just Freestyle My Visit?

Why Does This Trip Matter To Me?

I Plan To Learn:

Trip Name:

Location: Arrival Date: Arrival Time: End Of Trip Date:

During This Trip, I Felt: Best Memory Of The Trip:

Foods And Drinks I Enjoyed: I Am Now Inspired To:

Places I Have Visited: What I Would Recommend/Not
                                      Recommend About This Trip:

What I Enjoyed During My Trip: Would I Come Here Again?

What I Did Not Enjoy During My Trip: I Realized:

I Met:

My Trip Story:

Attach Picture

Off To My Next Adventure

Date: My Level Of Excitement:

I Am Naming This Trip:

Where Am I Going?

Who Am I Going With?

How Long Is This Trip?

I Plan To Travel By:

Any Layovers Or Detours On This Trip?

If Yes To The Previous Prompt, Where And Why?

Why Does This Trip Matter To Me?

Where Will I Be Staying?

The Reason For This Trip:

My Trip Budget:

I Want To See:

A Top Priority For Me On This Trip:

I Want To Experience:

Will I Have An Itinerary For This Trip Or Will I Just Freestyle My Visit?

I Plan To Learn:

Trip Name:

Location: Arrival Date: Arrival Time: End Of Trip Date:

During This Trip, I Felt:

Best Memory Of The Trip:

Foods And Drinks I Enjoyed:

I Am Now Inspired To:

Places I Have Visited:

What I Would Recommend/Not Recommend About This Trip:

What I Enjoyed During My Trip:

Would I Come Here Again?

What I Did Not Enjoy During My Trip:

I Realized:

I Met:

Attach Picture

My Trip Story:

Off To My Next Adventure

Date: My Level Of Excitement:

I Am Naming This Trip:

Where Will I Be Staying?

Where Am I Going?

The Reason For This Trip:

Who Am I Going With?

My Trip Budget:

How Long Is This Trip?

I Want To See:

I Plan To Travel By:

A Top Priority For Me On This Trip:

Any Layovers Or Detours On This Trip?

I Want To Experience:

If Yes To The Previous Prompt, Where And Why?

Will I Have An Itinerary For This Trip Or Will I Just Freestyle My Visit?

Why Does This Trip Matter To Me?

I Plan To Learn:

Trip Name:

Location: Arrival Date: Arrival Time: End Of Trip Date:

During This Trip, I Felt: Best Memory Of The Trip:

Foods And Drinks I Enjoyed: I Am Now Inspired To:

Places I Have Visited: What I Would Recommend/Not
                                             Recommend About This Trip:

What I Enjoyed During My Trip: Would I Come Here Again?

What I Did Not Enjoy During My Trip: I Realized:

I Met:

My Trip Story:

Attach Picture

Off To My Next Adventure

Date: My Level Of Excitement:

I Am Naming This Trip:

Where Will I Be Staying?

Where Am I Going?

The Reason For This Trip:

Who Am I Going With?

My Trip Budget:

How Long Is This Trip?

I Want To See:

I Plan To Travel By:

A Top Priority For Me On This Trip:

Any Layovers Or Detours On This Trip?

I Want To Experience:

If Yes To The Previous Prompt, Where And Why?

Will I Have An Itinerary For This Trip Or Will I Just Freestyle My Visit?

Why Does This Trip Matter To Me?

I Plan To Learn:

Trip Name:

Location: Arrival Date: Arrival Time: End Of Trip Date:

During This Trip, I Felt: Best Memory Of The Trip:

Foods And Drinks I Enjoyed: I Am Now Inspired To:

Places I Have Visited: What I Would Recommend/Not
                                              Recommend About This Trip:

What I Enjoyed During My Trip: Would I Come Here Again?

What I Did Not Enjoy During My Trip: I Realized:

I Met:

My Trip Story:

Attach Picture

You Can Find Me On Someone's Beach.

Traveling Is Self-Care.

Off To My Next Adventure

Date: _____ My Level Of Excitement:

I Am Naming This Trip:

Where Am I Going?

Who Am I Going With?

How Long Is This Trip?

I Plan To Travel By:

Any Layovers Or Detours On This Trip?

If Yes To The Previous Prompt, Where And Why?

Why Does This Trip Matter To Me?

Where Will I Be Staying?

The Reason For This Trip:

My Trip Budget:

I Want To See:

A Top Priority For Me On This Trip:

I Want To Experience:

Will I Have An Itinerary For This Trip Or Will I Just Freestyle My Visit?

I Plan To Learn:

Trip Name:

Location: Arrival Date: Arrival Time: End Of Trip Date:

During This Trip, I Felt: Best Memory Of The Trip:

Foods And Drinks I Enjoyed: I Am Now Inspired To:

Places I Have Visited: What I Would Recommend/Not
                                          Recommend About This Trip:

What I Enjoyed During My Trip: Would I Come Here Again?

What I Did Not Enjoy During My Trip: I Realized:

I Met:

Attach Picture

My Trip Story:

Off To My Next Adventure

Date: My Level Of Excitement: 😍   😄   😕   😱

I Am Naming This Trip:

Where Will I Be Staying?

Where Am I Going?

The Reason For This Trip:

Who Am I Going With?

My Trip Budget:

How Long Is This Trip?

I Want To See:

I Plan To Travel By:

A Top Priority For Me On This Trip:

Any Layovers Or Detours On This Trip?

I Want To Experience:

If Yes To The Previous Prompt, Where And Why?

Will I Have An Itinerary For This Trip Or Will I Just Freestyle My Visit?

Why Does This Trip Matter To Me?

I Plan To Learn:

Trip Name:

Location: Arrival Date: Arrival Time: End Of Trip Date:

During This Trip, I Felt: Best Memory Of The Trip:

Foods And Drinks I Enjoyed: I Am Now Inspired To:

Places I Have Visited: What I Would Recommend/Not
                                      Recommend About This Trip:

What I Enjoyed During My Trip: Would I Come Here Again?

What I Did Not Enjoy During My Trip: I Realized:

I Met:

Attach Picture

My Trip Story:

Off To My Next Adventure

Date: My Level Of Excitement:

I Am Naming This Trip:

Where Will I Be Staying?

Where Am I Going?

The Reason For This Trip:

Who Am I Going With?

My Trip Budget:

How Long Is This Trip?

I Want To See:

I Plan To Travel By:

A Top Priority For Me On This Trip:

Any Layovers Or Detours On This Trip?

I Want To Experience:

If Yes To The Previous Prompt, Where And Why?

Will I Have An Itinerary For This Trip Or Will I Just Freestyle My Visit?

Why Does This Trip Matter To Me?

I Plan To Learn:

Trip Name:

Location: Arrival Date: Arrival Time: End Of Trip Date:

During This Trip, I Felt: Best Memory Of The Trip:

Foods And Drinks I Enjoyed: I Am Now Inspired To:

Places I Have Visited: What I Would Recommend/Not Recommend About This Trip:

What I Enjoyed During My Trip: Would I Come Here Again?

What I Did Not Enjoy During My Trip: I Realized:

I Met:

Attach Picture

My Trip Story:

Traveling Makes You A Wonderful Storyteller.

The Goal:
To Travel
Mind,
Body,
And Spirit.

Off To My Next Adventure

Date: _____   My Level Of Excitement: 😇 😁 😝 😱

I Am Naming This Trip:

Where Am I Going?

Who Am I Going With?

How Long Is This Trip?

I Plan To Travel By:

Any Layovers Or Detours On This Trip?

If Yes To The Previous Prompt, Where And Why?

Why Does This Trip Matter To Me?

Where Will I Be Staying?

The Reason For This Trip:

My Trip Budget:

I Want To See:

A Top Priority For Me On This Trip:

I Want To Experience:

Will I Have An Itinerary For This Trip Or Will I Just Freestyle My Visit?

I Plan To Learn:

Trip Name:

Location: Arrival Date: Arrival Time: End Of Trip Date:

During This Trip, I Felt:

Best Memory Of The Trip:

Foods And Drinks I Enjoyed:

I Am Now Inspired To:

Places I Have Visited:

What I Would Recommend/Not Recommend About This Trip:

What I Enjoyed During My Trip:

Would I Come Here Again?

What I Did Not Enjoy During My Trip:

I Realized:

I Met:

Attach Picture

My Trip Story:

Off To My Next Adventure

Date: _____ My Level Of Excitement:

I Am Naming This Trip:

Where Will I Be Staying?

Where Am I Going?

The Reason For This Trip:

Who Am I Going With?

My Trip Budget:

How Long Is This Trip?

I Want To See:

I Plan To Travel By:

A Top Priority For Me On This Trip:

Any Layovers Or Detours On This Trip?

I Want To Experience:

If Yes To The Previous Prompt, Where And Why?

Will I Have An Itinerary For This Trip Or Will I Just Freestyle My Visit?

Why Does This Trip Matter To Me?

I Plan To Learn:

Trip Name:

Location: Arrival Date: Arrival Time: End Of Trip Date:

During This Trip, I Felt: Best Memory Of The Trip:

Foods And Drinks I Enjoyed: I Am Now Inspired To:

Places I Have Visited: What I Would Recommend/Not
                                        Recommend About This Trip:

What I Enjoyed During My Trip: Would I Come Here Again?

What I Did Not Enjoy During My Trip: I Realized:

I Met:

My Trip Story:

Attach Picture

Off To My Next Adventure

Date: My Level Of Excitement: 😊 😄 😌 😲

I Am Naming This Trip:

Where Am I Going?

Who Am I Going With?

How Long Is This Trip?

I Plan To Travel By:

Any Layovers Or Detours On This Trip?

If Yes To The Previous Prompt, Where And Why?

Why Does This Trip Matter To Me?

Where Will I Be Staying?

The Reason For This Trip:

My Trip Budget:

I Want To See:

A Top Priority For Me On This Trip:

I Want To Experience:

Will I Have An Itinerary For This Trip Or Will I Just Freestyle My Visit?

I Plan To Learn:

Trip Name:

Location: Arrival Date: Arrival Time: End Of Trip Date:

During This Trip, I Felt:

Best Memory Of The Trip:

Foods And Drinks I Enjoyed:

I Am Now Inspired To:

Places I Have Visited:

What I Would Recommend/Not Recommend About This Trip:

What I Enjoyed During My Trip:

Would I Come Here Again?

What I Did Not Enjoy During My Trip:

I Realized:

I Met:

My Trip Story:

Attach Picture

The
Whole
World
Is My
Home.

The Most Liberating Experience Is Traveling Alone.

Off To My Next Adventure

Date: _____ My Level Of Excitement:

I Am Naming This Trip:	Where Will I Be Staying?
Where Am I Going?	The Reason For This Trip:
Who Am I Going With?	My Trip Budget:
How Long Is This Trip?	I Want To See:
I Plan To Travel By:	A Top Priority For Me On This Trip:
Any Layovers Or Detours On This Trip?	I Want To Experience:
If Yes To The Previous Prompt, Where And Why?	Will I Have An Itinerary For This Trip Or Will I Just Freestyle My Visit?
Why Does This Trip Matter To Me?	I Plan To Learn:

Trip Name:

Location: Arrival Date: Arrival Time: End Of Trip Date:

During This Trip, I Felt: Best Memory Of The Trip:

Foods And Drinks I Enjoyed: I Am Now Inspired To:

Places I Have Visited: What I Would Recommend/Not
                                          Recommend About This Trip:

What I Enjoyed During My Trip: Would I Come Here Again?

What I Did Not Enjoy During My Trip: I Realized:

I Met:

Attach Picture

My Trip Story:

Off To My Next Adventure

Date: My Level Of Excitement:

I Am Naming This Trip:

Where Will I Be Staying?

Where Am I Going?

The Reason For This Trip:

Who Am I Going With?

My Trip Budget:

How Long Is This Trip?

I Want To See:

I Plan To Travel By:

A Top Priority For Me On This Trip:

Any Layovers Or Detours On This Trip?

I Want To Experience:

If Yes To The Previous Prompt, Where And Why?

Will I Have An Itinerary For This Trip Or Will I Just Freestyle My Visit?

Why Does This Trip Matter To Me?

I Plan To Learn:

Trip Name:

Location: Arrival Date: Arrival Time: End Of Trip Date:

During This Trip, I Felt: Best Memory Of The Trip:

Foods And Drinks I Enjoyed: I Am Now Inspired To:

Places I Have Visited: What I Would Recommend/Not
                                           Recommend About This Trip:

What I Enjoyed During My Trip: Would I Come Here Again?

What I Did Not Enjoy During My Trip: I Realized:

I Met:

My Trip Story:

Attach Picture

Off To My Next Adventure

Date: My Level Of Excitement: 😊 😄 😖 😱

I Am Naming This Trip:

Where Will I Be Staying?

Where Am I Going?

The Reason For This Trip:

Who Am I Going With?

My Trip Budget:

How Long Is This Trip?

I Want To See:

I Plan To Travel By:

A Top Priority For Me On This Trip:

Any Layovers Or Detours On This Trip?

I Want To Experience:

If Yes To The Previous Prompt, Where And Why?

Will I Have An Itinerary For This Trip Or Will I Just Freestyle My Visit?

Why Does This Trip Matter To Me?

I Plan To Learn:

Trip Name:

Location: Arrival Date: Arrival Time: End Of Trip Date:

During This Trip, I Felt: Best Memory Of The Trip:

Foods And Drinks I Enjoyed: I Am Now Inspired To:

Places I Have Visited: What I Would Recommend/Not
                                          Recommend About This Trip:

What I Enjoyed During My Trip: Would I Come Here Again?

What I Did Not Enjoy During My Trip: I Realized:

I Met:

Attach Picture

My Trip Story:

Wonderful Encounters I Have Experienced....

Next Stop: To The Moon

Off To My Next Adventure

Date: My Level Of Excitement:

I Am Naming This Trip:

Where Will I Be Staying?

Where Am I Going?

The Reason For This Trip:

Who Am I Going With?

My Trip Budget:

How Long Is This Trip?

I Want To See:

I Plan To Travel By:

A Top Priority For Me On This Trip:

Any Layovers Or Detours On This Trip?

I Want To Experience:

If Yes To The Previous Prompt, Where And Why?

Will I Have An Itinerary For This Trip Or Will I Just Freestyle My Visit?

Why Does This Trip Matter To Me?

I Plan To Learn:

Trip Name:

Location: Arrival Date: Arrival Time: End Of Trip Date:

During This Trip, I Felt:

Best Memory Of The Trip:

Foods And Drinks I Enjoyed:

I Am Now Inspired To:

Places I Have Visited:

What I Would Recommend/Not Recommend About This Trip:

Attach Picture

What I Enjoyed During My Trip:

Would I Come Here Again?

What I Did Not Enjoy During My Trip:

I Realized:

I Met:

My Trip Story:

Off To My Next Adventure

Date: _____   My Level Of Excitement: 😍 😃 😟 😱

I Am Naming This Trip:

Where Will I Be Staying?

Where Am I Going?

The Reason For This Trip:

Who Am I Going With?

My Trip Budget:

How Long Is This Trip?

I Want To See:

I Plan To Travel By:

A Top Priority For Me On This Trip:

Any Layovers Or Detours On This Trip?

I Want To Experience:

If Yes To The Previous Prompt, Where And Why?

Will I Have An Itinerary For This Trip Or Will I Just Freestyle My Visit?

Why Does This Trip Matter To Me?

I Plan To Learn:

Trip Name:

Location: Arrival Date: Arrival Time: End Of Trip Date:

During This Trip, I Felt:

Best Memory Of The Trip:

Foods And Drinks I Enjoyed:

I Am Now Inspired To:

Places I Have Visited:

What I Would Recommend/Not Recommend About This Trip:

What I Enjoyed During My Trip:

Would I Come Here Again?

What I Did Not Enjoy During My Trip:

I Realized:

I Met:

My Trip Story:

Attach Picture

277

Off To My Next Adventure

Date: My Level Of Excitement:

I Am Naming This Trip:

Where Will I Be Staying?

Where Am I Going?

The Reason For This Trip:

Who Am I Going With?

My Trip Budget:

How Long Is This Trip?

I Want To See:

I Plan To Travel By:

A Top Priority For Me On This Trip:

Any Layovers Or Detours On This Trip?

I Want To Experience:

If Yes To The Previous Prompt, Where And Why?

Will I Have An Itinerary For This Trip Or Will I Just Freestyle My Visit?

Why Does This Trip Matter To Me?

I Plan To Learn:

Trip Name:

Location: Arrival Date: Arrival Time: End Of Trip Date:

During This Trip, I Felt: Best Memory Of The Trip:

Foods And Drinks I Enjoyed: I Am Now Inspired To:

Places I Have Visited: What I Would Recommend/Not Recommend About This Trip:

What I Enjoyed During My Trip: Would I Come Here Again?

What I Did Not Enjoy During My Trip: I Realized:

I Met:

My Trip Story:

Attach Picture

Run
Away
With
Me.

I Love To See All Of God's Wonders.

Off To My Next Adventure

Date: _____ My Level Of Excitement: 😍 😁 😵‍💫 😱

I Am Naming This Trip:

Where Will I Be Staying?

Where Am I Going?

The Reason For This Trip:

Who Am I Going With?

My Trip Budget:

How Long Is This Trip?

I Want To See:

I Plan To Travel By:

A Top Priority For Me On This Trip:

Any Layovers Or Detours On This Trip?

I Want To Experience:

If Yes To The Previous Prompt, Where And Why?

Will I Have An Itinerary For This Trip Or Will I Just Freestyle My Visit?

Why Does This Trip Matter To Me?

I Plan To Learn:

Trip Name:

Location: Arrival Date: Arrival Time: End Of Trip Date:

During This Trip, I Felt: Best Memory Of The Trip:

Foods And Drinks I Enjoyed: I Am Now Inspired To:

Places I Have Visited: What I Would Recommend/Not
                                      Recommend About This Trip:

What I Enjoyed During My Trip: Would I Come Here Again?

What I Did Not Enjoy During My Trip: I Realized:

I Met:

Attach Picture

My Trip Story:

Off To My Next Adventure

Date: My Level Of Excitement:

I Am Naming This Trip:

Where Will I Be Staying?

Where Am I Going?

The Reason For This Trip:

Who Am I Going With?

My Trip Budget:

How Long Is This Trip?

I Want To See:

I Plan To Travel By:

A Top Priority For Me On This Trip:

Any Layovers Or Detours On This Trip?

I Want To Experience:

If Yes To The Previous Prompt, Where And Why?

Will I Have An Itinerary For This Trip Or Will I Just Freestyle My Visit?

Why Does This Trip Matter To Me?

I Plan To Learn:

Trip Name:

Location: Arrival Date: Arrival Time: End Of Trip Date:

During This Trip, I Felt: Best Memory Of The Trip:

Foods And Drinks I Enjoyed: I Am Now Inspired To:

Places I Have Visited: What I Would Recommend/Not
                                             Recommend About This Trip:

What I Enjoyed During My Trip: Would I Come Here Again?

What I Did Not Enjoy During My Trip: I Realized:

I Met:

My Trip Story:

Attach Picture

Traveling Makes You Richer.

Carpe Diem.

Off To My Next Adventure

Date: My Level Of Excitement: 😍 😁 🥹 😱

I Am Naming This Trip:

Where Will I Be Staying?

Where Am I Going?

The Reason For This Trip:

Who Am I Going With?

My Trip Budget:

How Long Is This Trip?

I Want To See:

I Plan To Travel By:

A Top Priority For Me On This Trip:

Any Layovers Or Detours On This Trip?

I Want To Experience:

If Yes To The Previous Prompt, Where And Why?

Will I Have An Itinerary For This Trip Or Will I Just Freestyle My Visit?

Why Does This Trip Matter To Me?

I Plan To Learn:

Trip Name:

Location: Arrival Date: Arrival Time: End Of Trip Date:

During This Trip, I Felt: Best Memory Of The Trip:

Foods And Drinks I Enjoyed: I Am Now Inspired To:

Places I Have Visited: What I Would Recommend/Not
                                      Recommend About This Trip:

What I Enjoyed During My Trip: Would I Come Here Again?

What I Did Not Enjoy During My Trip: I Realized:

I Met:

Attach Picture

My Trip Story:

Off To My Next Adventure

Date: My Level Of Excitement:

I Am Naming This Trip:

Where Will I Be Staying?

Where Am I Going?

The Reason For This Trip:

Who Am I Going With?

My Trip Budget:

How Long Is This Trip?

I Want To See:

I Plan To Travel By:

A Top Priority For Me On This Trip:

Any Layovers Or Detours On This Trip?

I Want To Experience:

If Yes To The Previous Prompt, Where And Why?

Will I Have An Itinerary For This Trip Or Will I Just Freestyle My Visit?

Why Does This Trip Matter To Me?

I Plan To Learn:

Trip Name:

Location: Arrival Date: Arrival Time: End Of Trip Date:

During This Trip, I Felt:

Foods And Drinks I Enjoyed:

Places I Have Visited:

What I Enjoyed During My Trip:

What I Did Not Enjoy During My Trip:

I Met:

Best Memory Of The Trip:

I Am Now Inspired To:

What I Would Recommend/Not Recommend About This Trip:

Would I Come Here Again?

I Realized:

Attach Picture

My Trip Story:

Fun Facts I Have Learned While Traveling....

Explore Your Home, Your City, Your Country, Your World.

Off To My Next Adventure

Date: My Level Of Excitement:

I Am Naming This Trip:

Where Will I Be Staying?

Where Am I Going?

The Reason For This Trip:

Who Am I Going With?

My Trip Budget:

How Long Is This Trip?

I Want To See:

I Plan To Travel By:

A Top Priority For Me On This Trip:

Any Layovers Or Detours On This Trip?

I Want To Experience:

If Yes To The Previous Prompt, Where And Why?

Will I Have An Itinerary For This Trip Or Will I Just Freestyle My Visit?

Why Does This Trip Matter To Me?

I Plan To Learn:

Trip Name:

Location: Arrival Date: Arrival Time: End Of Trip Date:

During This Trip, I Felt: Best Memory Of The Trip:

Foods And Drinks I Enjoyed: I Am Now Inspired To:

Places I Have Visited: What I Would Recommend/Not
                                      Recommend About This Trip:

What I Enjoyed During My Trip: Would I Come Here Again?

What I Did Not Enjoy During My Trip: I Realized:

I Met:

My Trip Story:

Attach Picture

Off To My Next Adventure

Date: My Level Of Excitement:

I Am Naming This Trip:

Where Will I Be Staying?

Where Am I Going?

The Reason For This Trip:

Who Am I Going With?

My Trip Budget:

How Long Is This Trip?

I Want To See:

I Plan To Travel By:

A Top Priority For Me On This Trip:

Any Layovers Or Detours On This Trip?

I Want To Experience:

If Yes To The Previous Prompt, Where And Why?

Will I Have An Itinerary For This Trip Or Will I Just Freestyle My Visit?

Why Does This Trip Matter To Me?

I Plan To Learn:

Trip Name:

Location: Arrival Date: Arrival Time: End Of Trip Date:

During This Trip, I Felt: Best Memory Of The Trip:

Foods And Drinks I Enjoyed: I Am Now Inspired To:

Places I Have Visited: What I Would Recommend/Not
                                           Recommend About This Trip:

What I Enjoyed During My Trip: Would I Come Here Again?

What I Did Not Enjoy During My Trip: I Realized:

I Met:

My Trip Story:

Attach Picture

My Travel Notes

Local Trips I Have Taken That I Would Recommend To Anybody....

Off To My Next Adventure

Date: My Level Of Excitement: 😍 😄 😬 😱

I Am Naming This Trip:

Where Will I Be Staying?

Where Am I Going?

The Reason For This Trip:

Who Am I Going With?

My Trip Budget:

How Long Is This Trip?

I Want To See:

I Plan To Travel By:

A Top Priority For Me On This Trip:

Any Layovers Or Detours On This Trip?

I Want To Experience:

If Yes To The Previous Prompt, Where And Why?

Will I Have An Itinerary For This Trip Or Will I Just Freestyle My Visit?

Why Does This Trip Matter To Me?

I Plan To Learn:

Trip Name:

Location: Arrival Date: Arrival Time: End Of Trip Date:

During This Trip, I Felt: Best Memory Of The Trip:

Foods And Drinks I Enjoyed: I Am Now Inspired To:

Places I Have Visited: What I Would Recommend/Not
                                                Recommend About This Trip:

What I Enjoyed During My Trip: Would I Come Here Again?

What I Did Not Enjoy During My Trip: I Realized:

I Met:

My Trip Story:

Attach Picture

Off To My Next Adventure

Date: My Level Of Excitement:

I Am Naming This Trip:

Where Will I Be Staying?

Where Am I Going?

The Reason For This Trip:

Who Am I Going With?

My Trip Budget:

How Long Is This Trip?

I Want To See:

I Plan To Travel By:

A Top Priority For Me On This Trip:

Any Layovers Or Detours On This Trip?

I Want To Experience:

If Yes To The Previous Prompt, Where And Why?

Will I Have An Itinerary For This Trip Or Will I Just Freestyle My Visit?

Why Does This Trip Matter To Me?

I Plan To Learn:

Trip Name:

Location: Arrival Date: Arrival Time: End Of Trip Date:

During This Trip, I Felt: Best Memory Of The Trip:

Foods And Drinks I Enjoyed: I Am Now Inspired To:

Places I Have Visited: What I Would Recommend/Not
Recommend About This Trip:

What I Enjoyed During My Trip: Would I Come Here Again?

What I Did Not Enjoy During My Trip: I Realized:

I Met:

Attach Picture

My Trip Story:

Off To My Next Adventure

Date: My Level Of Excitement:

I Am Naming This Trip:	Where Will I Be Staying?
Where Am I Going?	The Reason For This Trip:
Who Am I Going With?	My Trip Budget:
How Long Is This Trip?	I Want To See:
I Plan To Travel By:	A Top Priority For Me On This Trip:
Any Layovers Or Detours On This Trip?	I Want To Experience:
If Yes To The Previous Prompt, Where And Why?	Will I Have An Itinerary For This Trip Or Will I Just Freestyle My Visit?
Why Does This Trip Matter To Me?	I Plan To Learn:

Trip Name:

Location: Arrival Date: Arrival Time: End Of Trip Date:

During This Trip, I Felt:

Best Memory Of The Trip:

Foods And Drinks I Enjoyed:

I Am Now Inspired To:

Places I Have Visited:

What I Would Recommend/Not Recommend About This Trip:

What I Enjoyed During My Trip:

Would I Come Here Again?

What I Did Not Enjoy During My Trip:

I Realized:

I Met:

Attach Picture

My Trip Story:

Traveling List: Everywhere

Made in the USA
Columbia, SC
23 September 2023